Herb Gardens

KAY N. SANECKI

NEW HANOVER COUNTY
PUBLIC LIBRARY
201 CHESTNUT STREET
WILMINGTON, N. C. 28401

WARD LOCK

First published in Great Britain in 1994
by Ward Lock, Villiers House, 41/47 Strand,
London WC2N 5JE, England

A Cassell Imprint

Copyright © Ward Lock 1994

All rights reserved. No part of this publication may be
reproduced, stored in a retrieval system, or transmitted
in any form or by any means, electronic, mechanical,
photocopying, recording, or otherwise, without the
prior permission of the copyright owners.

British Library Cataloguing in Publication Data is
available upon application to The British Library

ISBN 0 7063 7212 3

Text filmset by Litho Link Ltd, Welshpool, Powys, Wales
Printed and bound in Singapore by Craft Print Pte Ltd

Previous page: **a terracotta
pot planted with variegated
thyme, common thyme and
box (*Buxus sempervirens*)
nicely complements a stone
bench.**

Contents

Preface

Herb gardens have a popular and universal appeal, not only for the many practical uses to which the plants can be put, but because they are undemanding plants and quite labour saving. Their economic value as flavouring for food, or as household remedies, scented items or insect repellents adds to the interest and satisfaction in growing them. The lovely gentle aromas of the summer herb garden are quite different to those of other kinds of gardens.

In the following pages many of the initial considerations in making a herb garden are discussed and some warnings of pitfalls are given. You are led step by step through initial approaches and helped to get the plans on to the ground. Gardens are not created overnight and you are shown that many preparations need to be undertaken before the plants are introduced; the book is arranged in the order of the work.

Growing herbs is a straightforward, reasonably easy form of gardening because the plants generally are able to look after themselves provided that the basic rules of garden hygiene are followed. Whether you are a beginner or a practised herb grower, you will find plenty of practical ideas in the pages that follow. Plans are put forward for both formal and informal gardens which should stimulate your imagination as to the possibilities in your own garden. Or, where a nucleus garden has already been established, you will be shown how to extend it or add appropriate features.

For those of you with little or no garden area, there are suggestions for growing herbs on balconies, in yards and on patios, and in window boxes and baskets. Some herbs can be cultivated indoors, so can be grown by flat dwellers or disabled gardeners.

Common names, with which many readers will be familiar, are used throughout the book, but the scientific name is also given to avoid any confusion. Common names in themselves are part of the interest of herbs but they vary from one locality to another and from one country to another. The A–Z of Herbs (see page 65) gives heights and descriptions and notes on the cultivation and uses of each plant.

Because herbs are ancient plants we tend to put them into 'period' gardens. This book looks back at Medieval garden styles and shows you how to adapt them for today in order to cultivate plants in the simplest ways possible. Knot gardens, an idea from the sixteenth century, are discussed and you are shown how to design your own. The book is presented as a guide through the various stages of embarking upon the making of a special garden which, once made, will give endless pleasure. K.N.S.

◄ A well-designed herb border with a variety of plants, some of which flow out over the path like pools.

ACKNOWLEDGEMENTS

The publishers would like to thank the following for
supplying photographs for this book: Pat Brindley:
pp. 80, 84; Garden Picture Library: pp. 9, 20, 24
(bottom), 25, 33, 36, 41, 49, 53, 60, 61, 68, 88; Jerry
Harpur: pp. 21, 24 (top), 48, 56; Iris Hardwick Picture
Library: pp. 8, 16, 17, 32, 37, 92; Clive Nichols: pp. 1,
28, 29, 40; Hugh Palmer: p. 52; Photos Horticultural
Picture Library: pp. 77, 85; Harry Smith: p. 4; Wildlife
Matters: p. 64.

The line illustrations were drawn by Vana Haggerty
F.L.S. and David Woodroffe.

· 1 ·
The World of Herbs

There is no doubt that considerable pleasure is to be derived from cultivating herbs and, because they are easy plants to grow, results can be encouraging. The word 'herb' comes from the Latin *herba* and since ancient times has meant a plant that serves a purpose – an economic plant.

Long before plants were cultivated in gardens for their decorative value, or before explorers risked their lives to bring back exciting new plants from the far corners of the earth, many of the ordinary plants that grew about were the ones that are now classed as herbs. These plants provided remedies and food flavouring, when no other products were available.

A BACKWARD GLANCE

The western world's knowledge of herbs grew out of the cultures of the ancient civilizations. Greek scholars compiled remarkable tomes concerning the qualities of herbs, that formed the basis of western medical practice for well over a thousand years. When the all-conquering Romans extended their empire over much of what we today call Europe, they took a number of their most useful plants with them to treat ailments, clean wounds and provide a few home comforts of life. Lavender and nettles, among other plants, were introduced to countries away from the Mediterranean in this way. Lavender was used in baths to cleanse and freshen the water; and nettles to chastize rheumaticky joints and ease the pain, and to provide spring greens.

Following the fall of the Roman Empire came the so-called Dark Ages, when plants remained vitally important domestic chattels, but knowledge of their value was simply being passed on by common usage. A clue to each plant's uses could be found in the common names which developed – for example, the plant used for eyes was eyebright, the plant to treat wounds, woundwort. Much of the folklore about herbs has its roots in these times, when important treatises were written by monks, each adding from their own personal experience or local knowledge of different plants.

Vast forests and uncharted heaths covered the land and represented the great unknown, believed to be the dwelling places of supernatural creatures. Great value was put on some plants as 'lucky charms', to protect and help not only the brave travellers but for the domestic protection and needs of human and animal life.

As Christianity spread through Europe, the monks and the church each played vital roles in popularizing herb lore. Ordinary people went to them to cure all manner of illnesses and injuries incurred during everyday life.

Early domestic use of herbs
There is evidence of herbs being cultivated within castle walls of the eleventh to fifteenth centuries,

sometimes as symbolic plants, frequently for remedies and flavouring, and sometimes amid turf to form what was called a 'flowery meade'. (The present–day popularity of a wild-flower meadow used as a conservation garden feature harks back to the Medieval period.)

Peasants who lived in humbler dwellings collected herbs from their local common lands for flavouring the potage (a thick soup), obscuring putrefaction and fermentation, staunching blood and providing divine protection. Success was often a hit and miss affair, but refinements were lacking; herbs were the only plants that were available and had to be brought into service. However, a full understanding of their uses still relied upon tradition.

The role of herbals

Meanwhile in monastries all over Europe the treatises written by the Greeks continued to be copied and re-copied, a smattering of further information being added here and there. Not until the invention of the printing press in the early fifteenth century and the realization that many of the plants previously recorded were natives of the Mediterranean basin, did knowledge spread and then only among the scholars. Herbals were among the first books to be printed and translated from Latin into French, high German and high Dutch.

In England a cleric named William Turner was the first to define many herbs, listing their names in several languages; then in the middle of the sixteenth century he produced the first herbal in English for ordinary people, so they could know their local plants and how to use them. He even coined new names where none existed before, names still recognized today. A few years later a standard European herbal of the time was translated into English by Henry Lyte who added observations for local plants (Somerset) and by the end of the century, in 1597, John Gerard published his herbal, which not only captured the imagination of the general literate population for the next 50 years, but has remained a favourite among herb growers.

The use of scent

The reign of Queen Elizabeth I of England (1558–1601) spanned the years in which many rich people began to cultivate plants for fun and make gardens for pleasure. This is the period when knot gardens were introduced and when the scent of plants was increasingly appreciated. Aromatic herbs had already provided flavour and remedies for ailments, but now they were strewn across floors in houses and on the earth floors of humbler

▲ In this attractive herb garden a formal, rectangular bed is literally boxed in and filled with colourful marigolds (*Calendula officinalis*).

▶ A knot garden can look most attractive set in old bricks and outlined in clipped box.

dwellings, in churches and public places to allay unhygienic smells and keep down flies, frogs and vermin. From now on scented herbs would be used commonly to sweeten linen, closets, to burn in chaffing dishes to scent candles and toilet waters, and above all to make pot-pourri (Fig. 1).

● *Pot-pourri* The term 'pot-pourri' has come to mean a mixture of dried scented flowers, aromatic leaves and spices. In the sixteenth century the idea was rather to preserve a moist mixture with what today would be called brandy. From the kitchen the remains of the cooking pot would be kept, and would include flowers like marigolds and pinks for flavour. A literal translation of pot-pourri is 'rotten pot'. Layers of scented flowers and leaves were preserved in salt to cure, dry and ferment them, and spices and perfume fixatives which were becoming more readily available

Fig. 1 A pot-pourri jar, such as would have been used in the sixteenth century.

were added. The result was known as 'sweet jar' while pot-pourri was moist. The pot-pourri of today has been developed from sweet jar and the plant material that can be put together and mixed successfully is infinite. Over the intervening centuries families have developed their own recipes. It was work for the women of the house along with the preparation of medicine, sweet waters, pomanders, sweet bags and vinegars.

Still-rooms
All this domestic work was carried out in the still-room, or distilling-room. Some of the wealthier households possessed small stills, whilst others purchased the plants' essential oils; but however grand or humble, the responsibility rested upon the ladies from Elizabethan times onward to maintain a stock of vital remedies, cosmetics, scented flavours, vinegars, waters, and preserves. Because both medicine and food often came from the same group plants, the still-rooms' recipe books embrace the complete range. Families developed their own favourite ideas. Over the years women have usually been the guardians of herbal lore.

Herbs and the New World
It was also during the last part of the sixteenth century that the floral and economic splendours of the North American continent became known. It was John Gerard's herbal and other important ones of the seventeenth century, notably John Parkinson's, that emigrants took with them to the New World. Just as the Romans had brought with them to a new land plants vital for their well-being, so the European settlers took dried herbs and seeds along with their pestle and mortar and their herbals as essentials. They learned new herbal traditions and plants from the native Indians, and gradually travellers brought

Essential oils

When 150 years ago a chemical experiment revealed the active principles of a herb – or vegetable drug as it was sometimes known – it became possible to synthesize medicines. Aspirin was among the first during the nineteenth century. These principles are the life-giving and aromatic ingredient within the essential oil, or essence of the plant.

Sometimes the scent is carried upon the air as with roses; otherwise it is locked into the fabric of the plant so that the tissue has to be bruised to release the aroma, as for bay (*Laurus nobilis*) used in cooking, or for mint (*Mentha* species) which is usually chopped. Sometimes a mere brush of the hand over a plant will release scented oil, as in rosemary (*Rosmarinus officinalis*).

The richness of the oil varies through the growing season of the plant and obviously it is best to harvest at a time when the oil is at its richest and most refined. Lavender (*Lavandula angustifolia*), harvested for the highest quality oil, is cut just as the flowers begin to open. In this case the time of harvesting is critical.

Experienced herb gardeners know that the mints (*Mentha* species) become rank once the plants have flowered. Other herbs, such as woodruff (*Galium odoratum*) only develop their fragrance after cutting and hold it well.

Coriander (*Coriandrum sativum*) changes its scent as the seed ripens, becoming sweeter and sweeter.

Various methods have been devised for extracting and preserving such oils, the most common is by distillation. Today essential oils can be purchased readily and are used in aromatherapy and homeopathy to treat the whole person – the scent itself playing a healing role.

---

plants home which became part of the herbal tradition of Europe, such as evening primrose (*Oenothera biennis*), echinacea (*Echinacea purpurea*), American poke (*Phytolacca americana*), Culver's root (*Leptandra virginiana*) and witch-hazel (*Hamamelis virginiana*).

By the mid seventeenth and into the eighteenth centuries more unfamiliar herbs and flowering plants were crossing the Atlantic ocean, brought by navigators and travellers and a great coterie of botanists and medical men, not only from the Americas but from other far-away places also. Physic gardens, later to be called botanic gardens were established, where medicinal plants could be studied.

Herbs for the people
Into this heightened activity and investigation of plants came a very popular herbal written by Nicholas Culpeper for the general population, which was widely read for more than a century. His *Doctrine of Signatures* adhered to an old Greek idea that plants indicated their intended use by some feature of their appearance. For example, the walnut resembles the human brain and was thus to be used for head injuries; or the milky splashes on lungwort suggested mucus and the treatment of chest infections.

Herbs in decline
Once medical and botanical knowledge advanced during the eighteenth and nineteenth centuries, ideas changed. Domestically the herbs remained important but their cultivation went unrecorded. Markets and apothecaries proliferated in the newly rising towns; pedlars and herb women still worked in the country areas. By the end of the nineteenth century, the cultivation of herbs was relegated to the kitchen garden and many fell out of use because of the growing popularity of proprietary sauces and relishes. Relatively few culinary herbs remained of importance.

Herbs revived

As the cultivation of herbs has increased a hundredfold since the late 1960s, many of them that had almost been lost to cultivation have been brought back. It has been an unplanned conservation exercise stimulated by a present-day occupation with heritage and because more and more people are turning to a holistic life-style. There is a charm, perhaps a humility about these modest plants that extravagantly flamboyant bedding and herbaceous plants lack.

Herb gardens today

During the last three decades the popularity of herb gardens has increased and designs and new ideas have developed. A herb garden, whatever the form or size, attracts attention because visitors examine and discuss the individual plants rather than the overall effect. A sense of relaxation and timelessness can be created among herbs and their marvellously varied aromas enjoyed, which lends them a charm beyond most other plants. In growing them and getting to know them, traditions are being continued. There is great satisfaction in growing the same simple plants unchanged by time that served man in the same way thousands of years ago.

In the following pages not only are ideas put forward for ways herbs can be enjoyed even without a garden (say on a balcony or around a mobile home), but step by step instructions are given for making a herb garden. Do not rush out and buy the plants; consider first the preparations, the site, the style, the funds and time available. The book has been planned in a practical way to lead the herb gardener to the right conclusions. Enjoy growing herbs!

◄ A random paved path leads towards a central fountain in a formal garden.

Herb names

Most gardeners know the country names of herbs which offer a clue to the former use of the plant: for example, woundwort, soapwort and eyebright. The first intent of the would-be herbalist should be to become familiar with the scientific names. Just as common names reveal clues, so do Latin names. As common names vary from one locality or country to another, the scientific name leaves no doubt universally as to the identity of a plant. Throughout the book Latin names are given, which offer more information about the plant: perhaps its use, its provenance or its habitat.

The first name is the generic or family name, thus all mints are *Mentha* and all marjorams *Origanum*, and the second or the specific name distinguishes the plant from all other members of its family. For example sage is *Salvia*, not one of the showy summer bedding kind or flowering perennials for the border but the one used in herbal medicine – the 'official' plant; thus it's called *officinalis*. As a specific name *officinalis*, when it occurs, always refers to a herb: rosemary is *Rosmarinus officinalis*, marigold is *Calendula officinalis* and vervain is *Verbena officinalis*. (These are not the names by which the previously mentioned herbalists knew the plants; the whole binomial system has only evolved since the eighteenth century.)

Not only are herbs simple plants but their Latin names are straightforward. Because they are less showy than flowering herbaceous plants they have avoided the attentions of the plant breeders in general and therefore, except in a small minority of instances, there are no deliberately cultivated varieties or cultivars. Familiar exceptions are the lavenders, like *Lavandula angustifolia* 'Hidcote' and thymes (*Thymus vulgaris* 'Silver Posie') or monarda (*Monarda didyma* 'Croftway Pink'). Otherwise the different forms that some herbs display have first been noticed and then developed by propagating vegetatively. This is how such plants as the painted sage *Salvia officinalis* 'Tricolor' have been produced.

· 2 ·
Planning a Herb Garden

Making a herb garden is not difficult provided one or two initial considerations are borne in mind. Whether you're thinking of growing useful culinary herbs or making a decorative centrepiece for your garden, it is the setting that is all-important. In particular, growing herbs successfully depends on three important factors: a suitable soil, some shelter from prevailing breezes and good light.

Soil

Soils vary from very sticky clays to dry and absorbent sands. Ideally herbs need something between, with a good humus content. Every soil can be improved in texture and quality by the addition of humus: it will make a soil more friable, allow water to penetrate more deeply and keep the soil temperature more equable between winter and summer. Any well-rotted vegetable or animal material becomes humus. Alternatively, a proprietary organic manure can be used at the recommended rates.

Your first task, when planning a herb garden, is to fork over the chosen area, preferably in the autumn, removing perennial weeds and adding some compost or other humus-producing material to improve the soil condition for the following season. Leave the surface rough to weather and dress it with an environmentally friendly residual weedkiller to control the annual weeds the following spring. If any levelling has to be done, ensure that the top soil remains as top soil by keeping it separate from the subsoil.

Shelter

Hedges and open fences have a considerable advantage over walls in providing shelter for herbs, because they sift the breeze rather than provide a barrier which creates strong eddies.

● *Hedges* Nothing is prettier than a hedge as a herb garden boundary. This can be informal and blowsy, or formal and clipped. The apothecary's rose (*Rosa gallica officinalis*) or rosemary (*Rosmarinus officinalis*), box (*Buxus sempervirens*) and bay (*Laurus nobilis*) are plants to consider for herb hedges, although bay and rosemary may not be entirely successful in colder areas. A lower-growing hedge can be formed of a number of herbs, perhaps backed by a fence if the site needs it. Lower internal hedges of this kind add structure and shape to the garden and again can be formally clipped as for wall germander (*Teucrium chamaedrys*) or lavender cotton (*Santolina* species) or left free-growing. Such herb hedges are not long-lived and will need to be renovated with fresh plants from time to time, or replanted entirely, say every five years or so. Some, such as those composed of southernwood (*Artemisia abrotanum*), curry plant (*Helichrysum serotinum*) or hyssop (*Hyssopus officinalis*) will look pretty drab

· HANDY TIP ·

Rustic screens, woven from willow and wire, take a little time to create but are well worth the effort. They form twiggy panels or arbours which blend readily and unobtrusively, sheltering and supporting plants and lending a timeless rusticity to herb gardens. Rural wicker screens and panels serve the same purpose.

in the winter months; although the entire herb garden offers little in the way of winter decorative effect.

● *Fences* can be both attractive and serviceable if they are of a pleasant design, and will go a long way to lending a feeling of enclosure and contentment to the herb garden, shutting out the outside world, as it were. Garden centres and builders' merchants offer a range of wood-preserving materials in attractive shades of brown, green and silver, so there is no need to have a fence that looks purely utilitarian. When fencing boards do not fit together tightly but allow a small space between, the breeze will be sifted and the fence is far less likely to be blown over in a gale. Taller plants often do well grown in front of a fence and are less prone to lean in the force of the prevailing breezes.

Wattle fencing panels or low fencing – a picket fence for example, will provide protection almost as effectively as taller fences and will contain leaning plants and provide a scrambling base for herbs like hops (*Humulus lupulus*) or jasmine (*Jasminum officinale*) to form a pretty flowering barrier. Resist the temptation to plant roses such as the sweetbriar (*Rosa rubiginosa*) against a wattle or loose-pannelled fence. The whippy

prickly growth will become entangled in the fence very quickly, making pruning a patience-testing task. Ultimately, the fence and rose will become an inseparable barrier.

● *Walls* Although arguably not as effective a form of shelter as a hedge or fence, there is no doubt that an attractive wall can still make a superb herb garden boundary (Fig. 2).

The reliability of any wall depends upon its foundation and the choice of building materials is often dictated by the type of the property and district. Low walls and 'dry' walls are popular in gardens, often constructed of stone, where plants can be tucked between and others planted along the top. Suitable herbs to tuck in to the wall itself are: houseleek (*Sempervivum tectorum*), hyssop (*Hyssopus officinalis*) and thyme (*Thymus* species), especially *T. vulgaris* and its cultivars. Herbs to grow along the top are many and the

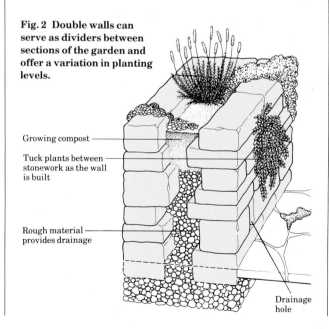

Fig. 2 Double walls can serve as dividers between sections of the garden and offer a variation in planting levels.

Growing compost

Tuck plants between stonework as the wall is built

Rough material provides drainage

Drainage hole

taller-growing ones are to be avoided, as are those that need a moist soil, such as the mints (*Mentha* species). Try lavenders (*Lavandula angustifolia*) and its low-growing cultivars, clove pinks (*Dianthus caryophyllus*), thymes, especially the creeping ones such as *Thymus serpyllum* and its forms, wall germander (*Teucrium chamaedrys*) and chives (*Allium schoenoprasm*).

Light

Good light is another essential for most herbs. Where a garden is overshadowed by trees, it is advisable not to attempt to cultivate herbs except perhaps in pots that can be relocated from time to time to take advantage of the light as the season progresses. If the tree canopy is light or can be thinned to give sunshine for several hours a day, then some herbs will grow. Those that are tolerant of semi-shade are indicated in the A–Z of Herbs (from page 65).

STYLE OF HERB GARDEN: FORMAL OR INFORMAL?

Having selected the best site for your herb garden in terms of soil, shelter and light, you are now ready to decide on the style your herb garden should take. Often the answer is governed by the space available or by the site itself. The simplest forms of herb gardens are usually allotted to a small space. They can be single blocks of planting, or pave and plant (see page 18) or, more likely, a corner of herbs. If this is so, select only a few herbs of varying height and form for the most pleasing effect.

◄ **Dramatic heads of angelica (*Angelica archangelica*) dominate a border backed by a wall.**

► **A tall yew hedge provides ample shelter for a large herb garden, in which honeysuckle (*Lonicera periclymenum*) grown as standards, adds height.**

Perhaps the size of the site or the immediate surroundings suggest a formal or geometric approach. Where a formal treatment is considered, it is more important to have a level site than for an informal garden, otherwise the sense of pattern will be lost. Formal gardens are more of a statement and require more of a contrived setting. The plan must be simple, as fussiness will end up as confusion once the plants become established. It is important that the size ought to relate to the garden as a whole. Think of it as putting a carpet in a room. You don't want it to be too small and be lost in the middle; neither do you want an overpoweringly busy pattern in a small area.

Simple ideas for a small formal herb bed

The earliest monastic gardens in which a wide selection of herbs was grown were based upon a sensible plan of rows of small rectangular beds with paths between. This was the pattern taken

up by the Medieval physic gardens (later to become early botanic gardens) and it was supremely practical. Only one sort of plant was grown in each small bed, it could be tended easily from all sides and, once harvested, something else could be planted without disturbing other plants. Some sort of crop rotation could be practised, whereby the position of plants is changed yearly so that before pests and diseases can build up to damaging levels in one area, you will have planted a new, unrelated plant which is not susceptible.

● *Pave and plant* is a modern variation on the above (Fig. 3). Expense of paving apart, it has the advantage of covering an area well, needing relatively little upkeep, and of being versatile. You could, for example, lay ten paving slabs one year and ten more the following season as funds allow, and these could cross an area from say, the garage to the house, or from a patio to a vegetable garden. Provided that there is sufficient light, it could link any one part of the garden with another.

Fig. 3 Pave and plant is an effective way of showing individual herbs, each in its own planting area.

Chequer-board design, as this is usually called today, is a good way to start growing herbs. Each square soil space is filled with just one kind of herb, which means that through a season you can more easily assess the progress of the plant and become familiar with any foibles. Try a culinary chequer-board, where only those herbs used in the kitchen are planted.

One word of caution: unless the site is fairly extensive, large-growing herbs such as angelica (*Angelica archangelica*) would tend to be out of proportion. Where the location allows, it is better to keep taller herbs to one side rather than dot them about the area, and it will make the 'garden' easier to manage.

● *A kitchen herb garden* (Fig. 4) based upon a grid system is ideal for a collection of culinary herbs. An alternative to the chequer-board design discussed earlier, this could comprise rows of long narrow borders. Not only does this look very neat, it makes the herbs very accessible. Some culinary herbs tend to become straggly and loll on their neighbour. In linear or rectangular beds of manageable size, these can be more easily controlled.

If wider straight-sided beds are made, they ought to be planted in blocks of each plant, with annuals sown in rows and thinned later to form a block.

● *A circular herb bed* can prove most attractive, but one cardinal rule which always bears repeating is not to arrange concentric rings. If the whole circle is comprised of rings they need to be broken up, either by pathways or by some formal edging plant that can be clipped, such as box (*Buxus sempervirens*) or lavender cotton (*Santolina* species). From a design aspect there should be a central feature which acts as a visual hub and, in a sense, pulls the whole plot together. A small statue, or perhaps a classical pot filled with

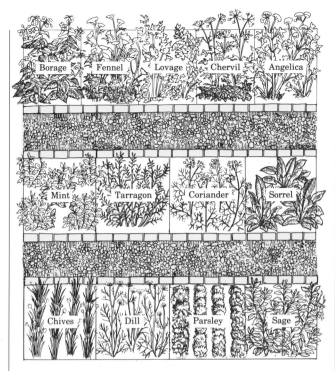

Fig. 4 Simple rows of block planting make an interesting experiment in herb cultivation for summer effect.

traditional herbs, or even an eye-catching standard plant, would all serve admirably.

An obvious variation of the circular bed is to make a series of circles like balloons linked with a repetitive theme of edging or edging tiles.

● *A wheel garden* is another simple idea for a small circular herb bed, or as a central feature for a more extensive garden. With spokes radiating from the centre as in a wheel, each wedge-shaped bed that is formed is filled with one kind of herb. Thus a scented wheel could be made using lavender (*Lavandula angustifolia*), lavender cotton (*Santolina* species) and thymes (*Thymus* species). Or you could try a medicinal wheel of peppermint (*Mentha* × *piperita*), lungwort (*Pulmonaria officinalis*), and hyssop (*Hyssopus officinalis*).

A further idea is to make a collection of

lavenders to fill the wedges of the bed, but inevitably towards the end of the season the shape of the wheel would be obscured by growth. The 'spokes' themselves need to be fairly wide in this case, perhaps formed of pebbles, small paving stones or, where a more permanent image is desired, of clipped box (wide enough to prevent the plants from leaning over one another).

The wheel idea also lends itself to a collection of thymes, where the ground-hugging plants can be clipped back to form a lovely cushion of a wheel.

● *Larger circles* Only when the circle is large can it effectively be cut up into four sections by crossed paths. When such a basic plan is carried out over a small area the finished garden looks like a hot cross bun, and soon becomes untidy.

When four beds are formed there needs to be a co-ordinating feature such as an edging of box (*Buxus sempervirens*) or wall germander (*Teucrium chamaedrys*). Then each bed could hold a collection of medicinal, culinary, scented or dye plants. The taller plants need to be set towards the outer rim of the circle to define the edge of the design.

● *The square garden* in its simplest guise might consist of four beds formed by two crossing paths, one north-south and the other east-west of the square. Each bed could hold a different group of herbs: the first, say, could be culinary; the second medicinal; the third, those used for dyeing; and the fourth 'folk-lore' plants such as periwinkle (*Vinca major*), ivy (*Hedera helix*), mullein (*Verbascum thapsus*) and monkshood (*Aconitum napellus*).

● *Combining a square and a circle* is the next stage in the geometric progress towards making a formal herb garden. To put a square inside a circle usually works far better than to make the circle the centre-piece. In the latter case, there is

◄ An unusual rectangular knot garden attractively surrounded by bricks forms a central feature.

► In carpet planting herbs are used in a formal way for a season.

often a tendency to have the square too near to the centre, crowding the curves of the circle or circles in the middle.

It is best to draw some ideas for the design on squared paper first. Then, when the plan looks right it can be transferred to the ground (Fig. 9 on page 39). Keep your ideas simple, and outline each bed with plants, tiles or wood to emphasize the shape and unity of the design.

For a garden of this kind it becomes obvious at once that paths have to be made and either paved or turved (see also Chapter 3). Stone paths are far less work in a small layout, where grass cutting

and edge trimming in a small garden can become the major chore. On the other hand, beds cut into an existing lawn can make an 'instant' garden ready to plant up in the spring. Hard paving has to be laid first in order to form the beds and may constitute a limiting factor on account of the cost. So turf paths could be replaced later by hard paving if desired.

Whatever you choose, remember to make any path wide enough: a well-proportioned path will enhance the character of the whole garden and, at the same time, more readily accommodate floppy and spreading plants.

DESIGNING A FORMAL HERB GARDEN

One of the attractions of the formal herb garden is the symmetry and rhythm of the design, with pathways wide enough to be distinguishable. The most elaborate formal designs are repetitive in some way, either one half or one quarter is a mirror image of the remainder, or circles or rings are set within borders or outlying beds. Each bed needs to be clearly outlined either by attractive edging tiles, bricks set on end boards or the same clipped plant, so that a unity is expressed within the design.

The reason behind growing herbs in a formal way is two-fold. Firstly the plants themselves can not generally be described as eyecatching, so the manner in which they are presented needs to be imaginative; secondly, herb gardens can somehow appear more authentic when planted as they were in years gone by, that is, in some geometric or straight-line fashion.

Smaller formal gardens are most attractive when low-growing plants themselves create the pattern, as in a knot garden.

Knot gardens

Knot gardens were first recorded in England in the fifteenth century, when household linen was spread out to dry on clipped lavender and rosemary to freshen it.

During the sixteenth century they became very popular, viewed almost as the diminutive version of the grand Renaissance garden. In those times the pattern or knot was designed to be looked at from above (usually a casement window). Today knot gardens consist of an elaborate arrangement of close-growing plants with clipped outlines.

Its success depends on being designed to the correct proportions, and regular maintenance. Although a knot appears to be complicated and intricate, the secret lies in using no more than three kinds of herb for the main outlines. Suitable plants from which to choose are: lavender cotton (*Santolina* species), thyme (*Thymus* species), wall germander (*Teucrium chamaedrys*), box (*Buxus sempervirens*) and dwarf lavenders (*Lavandula angustifolia* forms).

● *Pattern ideas* for simple knots can be found in the architecture, woodwork and embroidery of the sixteenth century. Most gardening books of the period offer design suggestions for 'a real knot', no rights or wrongs about the patterns. If there is one golden rule, it is that the smaller the area, the simpler the design ought to be.

● *Marking out* It's always a good idea to doodle any designs on squared paper first, in colour preferably, and label each ribbon of plants with the plant name. This will give a sense of scale if each square on the paper represents a given measurement on the ground.

Then, on your chosen site, mark out the square (or rectangle) for the knot garden and criss-cross it with garden lines extended between pegs, so that each square on the ground relates to a square on the paper. It should be a simple matter to transfer your design.

Alternatively, you can design directly on the ground by first marking out a square or rectangle the size of the proposed knot garden, and then 'designing' within it. To find the centre of the bed stretch diagonal cords from the corners; where they intersect will give mid-point. A peg driven in here with a cord attached can then be used like a compass to describe arcs or circles on the ground. Where straight lines are needed, either measure carefully at various points or put a plank across the design and draw along the side of it (Fig. 5).

Indicate the main lines with sand, trickled fairly liberally from a bottle or carton. At this point further or alternative arcs can then be described by putting a stake in at the halfway mark of one of the sides of the square and stretching the cord to the corner and making the arc to the other corner. You could try a number of variations.

An octagonal bed can be marked out by first drawing a square, taking care that the corners are right angles, then drawing four arcs from the corners using the distance to mid-point as radius. The points at which the arcs cut the square make the corners of the octagon. Leave the design for a couple of days and look at it critically from key viewing points (say, from the house). This way you should notice if any alterations need to be made before you begin planting.

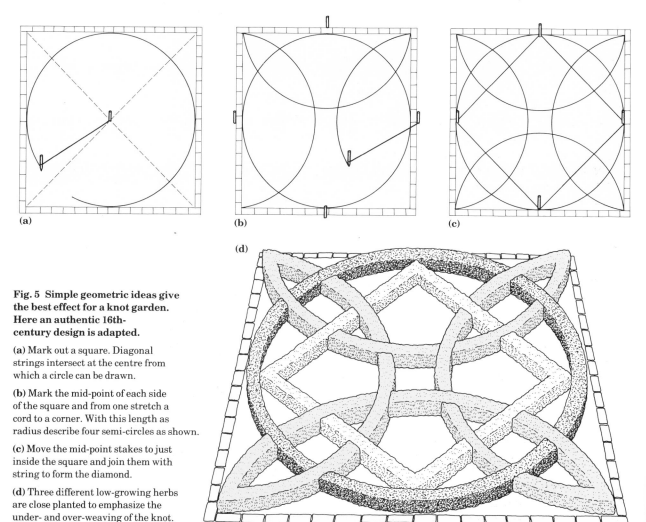

(a)

(b)

(c)

(d)

Fig. 5 Simple geometric ideas give the best effect for a knot garden. Here an authentic 16th-century design is adapted.

(a) Mark out a square. Diagonal strings intersect at the centre from which a circle can be drawn.

(b) Mark the mid-point of each side of the square and from one stretch a cord to a corner. With this length as radius describe four semi-circles as shown.

(c) Move the mid-point stakes to just inside the square and join them with string to form the diamond.

(d) Three different low-growing herbs are close planted to emphasize the under- and over-weaving of the knot.

23

◄ Barley sugar topiary in a simple formal arrangement of clipped box (*Buxus sempervirens*).

▼ Small formal beds set among brick paving give a colourful and pretty effect in this herb garden.

● *Planting* should begin in the spring. Decide which plant is going to form the major ribbon of the design – the one that will link the different areas of the knot garden through 'overlacing' and give it its sense of unity. Calculate the number of plants required and then, if you can afford it, try to get them in all at the same time from the same source (plus a few extra for the inevitable replacements which are bound to occur). Place the selected small plants very close together along the planting line, say 8–10 cm (3–4 in) apart in order to give a ribbon effect as soon as possible and to encourage plants to grow. Keep the plants well watered and sprayed until they are established; then as soon as possible clip them all back to about 15 cm (6 in) from the ground to help make them bushy. Remember to clip the sides of each plant as well, as a start towards training.

● *Aftercare* of a newly planted knot is a constant vigil and be prepared that it will take time to establish anything that resembles the desired effect. Clip the top sides of all the plants regularly to a uniform height, except at the intersections where the overlacing plant should be shaped to look as though it rises and crosses over the lower ribbon. If you have the space, keep a supply of the same plants in a nursery bed and clip them at the same time so that should they be needed for replacements, they will fit in well.

Spaces between the young plants need to be weeded regularly to keep the design clearly defined. Resist the temptation to plant up these spaces during the first year.

During the early stages they can be covered with pebbles or coloured shale in much the same manner as was done in the sixteenth century during the winter months. Small plants to use for

▶ **A path runs between an informal herb border and a crisp trellis-like planting of box (Buxus sempervirens).**

close planting later to enhance the pattern are: viola (*Viola* species), daisy (*Bellis perennis*), auricula (*Primula auricula*), thyme (*Thymus* species), dwarf-growing lavender (*Lavandula* cultivars), cowslip (*Primula veris*), purple-leaved plantain (*Plantago major* 'Rubrifolia') and the double-flowered chamomile (*Chameamelum nobile flore pleno*).

Open knots

Still working on a level site, an open knot style garden can be made where there is plenty of space. The design of an open knot can be identical to that of a knot, with the difference being that the ribbons are paths and so it is on a much grander scale. Each bed is outlined with a suitable low-growing herb or one that will tolerate clipping. The same herb should be used throughout to ensure uniformity of appearance. Useful edging herbs for this purpose are: wall germander (*Teucrium chamaedrys*), box (*Buxus sempervirens*), thyme (*Thymus* species), lavender cotton (*Santolina chamaecyparissus*) or chives (*Allium schoenoprasm*).

Marking out can be carried out in exactly the same way as for a knot (see page 22), using longer lines. Again, drawing the whole design out on squared paper first is the most accurate and labour-saving method, and will help to ensure symmetry. Keep the paths a uniform width and do not make them too wide, otherwise the effect will be lost.

Elaboration of a basic design such as described could be the starting point for a larger herb garden. Remember always to repeat a theme or shape at each side of the site to maintain an integrated and symmetrical design (see Chapter 4). A personal emblem or initials could also be included in the design, formed from an easily clipped plant.

DESIGNING AN INFORMAL HERB GARDEN

A simple border or bed planted informally with herbs is obviously the easiest and certainly the quickest way to establish a herb plot. However certain rules still need to be followed to give a satisfactory visual effect. Often the answer is governed by the site and the immediate surroundings. There may be shrub planting in the vicinity, or so-called 'village planting' of fruit trees and roses and vegetable patches. Both types of location beg for an informal herb garden.

The term 'informal planting' refers to the beds in which the plants are set. Unlike formal gardens, informal ones have no pattern on the ground as a starting point, but have a seemingly casual arrangement of plants.

● *A one-sided border,* such as a border backed by a house or garage wall, or a garden fence, may be all that is available. If so, keep the front edge irregular, whether this overlaps a lawn or path; forget about straight lines. Plan the planting in the fashion of an herbaceous border, the tallest plants at the back, the smallest at the front, and allow the medium-height ones to fill the space between. Set those of medium height in curves or groups, allowing some to come fairly near the front of the border so that the final visual effect will not be that of three stiff ranks. (The heights of herbs are given in the A–Z of Herbs in Chapter 7).

● *A two-sided border,* that is a border which is viewed from both sides (perhaps dividing a path from a lawn area) needs a different kind of planting. Visual success depends on the proportion of the width of the border to the height of the plants selected. A border alongside a path is looked down upon, so lower-growing herbs are more effective than bold clumps of elecampane (*Inula helenium*) or lovage (*Levisticum officinale*), unless the border is very wide.

The rule holds for putting the lowest and creeping plants towards the edge on either side of the border, and taller ones towards the centre. Break up the heights. (It may be useful to draw a planting plan on paper first, to ensure that there is an adequate mix of plants.) Resist the temptation to set a row of edging plants all along the path verge; instead choose groups of low-growing or spreading plants such as chives (*Allium schoenoprasm*), salad burnet (*Sanguisorba minor*), violets (*Viola* species) or painted sage (*Salvia officinalis* 'Tricolor').

● *An informal island bed* (Fig. 6) can be set in the lawn or paving, planted with the tallest plants towards the middle. Consider the proportions of the whole feature; Mugwort (*Artemisia vulgaris*) and goat's rue (*Galegia officinalis*) rarely look well in a small island bed. Again, make the outline irregular rather than a definite circle or oval. For a suburban garden a large teardrop shape often looks best, or perhaps two together or one mirroring another in shape.

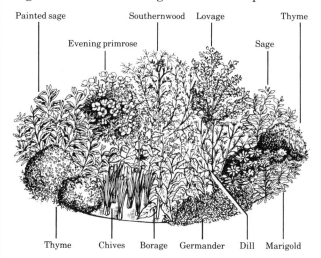

Painted sage   Southernwood   Lovage   Thyme

Evening primrose   Sage

Thyme   Chives   Borage   Germander   Dill   Marigold

Fig. 6 Herbs grown together in an island bed jostle for position in an informal way in summer.

● *A cottage-style herb garden,* where each plant grows uninhibited, is an ideal for which a considerable area is needed. It can best be achieved within an old walled garden or courtyard or perhaps in an old orchard. Let your imagination go but always remember that the essential quality and appeal of the cottage style is the controlled confusion.

It may be that a fairly haphazard garden has been inherited and can be tidied and transformed into a country style without clearing everything away. Many plants are justifiably included in wide-ranging herb gardens: plants to include in a cottage-style herb garden could be anything from crab apples to garlic so, with a modicum of flair, lovely tumbling borders can comprise peonies (*Paeonia officinalis*) roses (*Rosa* species), honesty (*Lunaria annua*), dame's violet (*Hesperis matrionalis*), irises (*Iris florentina, I. pseudacorus* and *I. foetidissima*), bugle (*Ajuga reptans*), rhubarb (*Rheum officinalis*) and yellow loosestrife (*Lysimachia vulgaris*). This will make a garden where generous clumps of plants jostle for position while sinuous hops and jasmines thread their way through. Not all the plants listed here are herbs, as we understand the term (although some will be harvested for scent or for culinary use), but who could resist such a sweet-smelling cornucopia of old-fashioned plants?

A major decision at the outset, whichever style of herb garden is chosen, is the amount of time available for the project. A profuse informal garden will need a lot of attention in the autumn when herbaceous stems need to be cut back and the top growth disposed of. You may want to devote time to harvesting and drying herbs (see page 66), and the risk with informal herb planting is that you can grow far more than you actually need or can use.

◀ Old railway sleepers form a low raised bed where herbs jostle together with other plants.

▶ A well-filled and pretty herb bed with a central sundial.

Basic Groundwork

Having reached some decision about the style and size your herb garden should take, and having marked out the design on the ground, the next step is to lay down the hard landscape areas of the garden with the best materials that funds allow, and then of course to start acquiring the all-important plants themselves.

Paths and paving

Time spent on the construction of paths or paved areas within a garden is always worth while. Not only do paths usually represent the skeleton or form of the garden, but they afford ease of access to the plants. Consider the texture and colour of the paving material, then make a rough estimate of the paved area to be covered and how much material will be required and this way the cost can be estimated fairly accurately.

Remember that paths need to be wide enough to allow a wheelbarrow to be taken along without damaging plants. Once herbs are established they will lean over the edges of paths, billowing into wavy forms that will reduce the width of the space. If you want to avoid having to negotiate your way through knee-high wet plants on rainy days, a minimum width of 75 cm (30 in) should be allowed for a working path.

● *Choosing the right materials* A straight path is easier to lay than a curved one, but where an informal setting for herbs requires curved walk-ways, then consider using gravel, chippings or stepping-stones so that a regular outline can be maintained, and avoid too many tight curves.

Whatever form a path takes, an edging of bricks or stones bedded into mortar, or edging tiles (some suitably 'old-fashioned' types are on the market again), or even wooden planks suitably preserved will prevent soil from washing over the path or invasive plants from encroaching. Even when edging plants are used, a firm path outline is a good idea.

A wide range of paving material is available from garden centres and building merchants but try to avoid brightly coloured slabs as these are unsympathetic to the gentle hues of herbs and present an anachronism alongside these ancient plants. Old bricks or street paving, or pebbles set in mortar can be used imaginatively without looking too busy. Where concrete is selected as the path material, brush or rake the surface while it is drying to eliminate the harshness and lend some tone and texture to the finished area.

Cobbles or stepping-stones bedded into the concrete or into mortar within, say, round, square or diamond-shape patches will help to break up the surface and maintain a sympathetic appearance (Fig. 7).

The same materials can be used for larger circulation areas within the herb garden and will look especially effective if spaces are left between the brick or stone setts in which to introduce herbs. Some herbs lend themselves particularly to being used in this way, and make attractive cushions or mats of growth.

● *Planting in paving* Introduce thymes (*Thymus* species) – some are mat-forming, others form little cushions of growth – chamomile (*Chamaemelum nobile*), feverfew (*Tanacetum parthenium*), hyssop (*Hyssopus officinalis*) chives (*Allium shoenoprasm*) and lavender cotton (*Santolina* species). In fact, not only herbs that will tolerate treading, but any that can be restrained and will not wander too far over the paving.

Gravel gardens

Gravel gardens offer the great advantage over normal soil gardens of being labour saving. Preparation is quite straightforward, provided that you have a level site and the light is good. First, clear all perennial weeds, fork over the ground and undertake any levelling; then cover the site with stout plastic sheeting. Cut holes into the sheeting where plants are to grow and push through a stake (preferably labelled) to indicate the correct position. Cover the site with clean gravel to a depth of 8 cm (3 in) and rake it over. Next, plant the herbs through the holes (which will be indicated by the stakes) by gently clearing the gravel around the stake, then returning it after planting. The sheeting will act as a weed barrier and a mulch, but if drainage becomes a problem in wet seasons, simply make a few extra holes in the plastic where the troublesome spots are. Herbs grown this way will not suffer from soil splashes!

▶ **Fig. 7 Paths are a vital part of garden design. Choose materials which complement the style of the house and garden and use mat-forming plants like thyme to soften the path edges.**

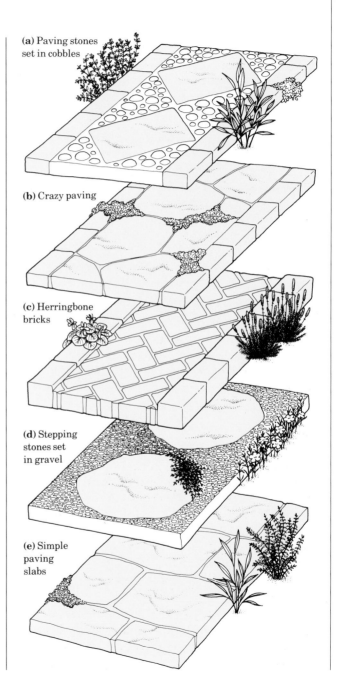

(a) Paving stones set in cobbles

(b) Crazy paving

(c) Herringbone bricks

(d) Stepping stones set in gravel

(e) Simple paving slabs

◀ Double-flowered chamomile (*Chamaemelum nobile* 'Flora Pleno') carpets the base of a chunky terracotta urn.

▶ A straw bee skep forms the point of interest in a small formal herb garden.

● *Decorative features* It is easy to think of decorative features as final touches to a new garden, when in fact to be truly effective as focal points, they need to be in place at a much earlier stage.

A garden on gravel needs a little more thought to bring the design together than a formal herb garden or a border set along a lush green lawn. Atmosphere will be achieved by first selecting a shade of gravel that blends well with any surrounding walls or buildings, and then by introducing some bold plants at various points such as elecampane (*Inula helenium*), lovage (*Levisticum officinale*), angelica (*Angelica archangelica*) or poke root (*Phytolacca americanum*) and allowing smaller herbs to huddle around their feet. One or two figures or classical jars carefully placed can help the form of the garden also. Some nurseries, herb nurseries in particular, offer quite sophisticated topiary work cut in box (*Buxus semper-*

virens) which could be displayed: globes or spirals resembling barley sugar twirls. Several are needed, set at intervals, to integrate the design.

Especially in a formal herb garden any decorative feature needs to be introduced with considerable care. An old item or at least one suggestive of age or heritage, such as a straw bee skep or millstone, will fit in far more sympathetically than a moulded figure fresh from the garden centre. A search through a market or an antique dealer's store might well reveal an old well-head, sundial, bird bath or fountain basin. Another suggestion is a decorative dripping cistern set against a side wall, 30–40 cm (12–16 in) high, perhaps in a D-shape to form a tank which is then waterproofed; the top edge set with smooth coping stones will serve as a seat or a table. (A seat of some kind is almost essential in a herb garden – after all, you want to be able to sit and enjoy your plants.)

Changing the ground level

A level site is vital if you want to show your herbs at their best, but on a very uneven ground where considerable earth moving might otherwise be needed, a sunken herb garden may offer the ideal solution. If a symmetrical shape can be made on a lower level area and steps made to enter it, perhaps on opposite sides, then the problem is overcome.

● *Steps* (Fig. 8) need very careful construction to achieve the correct proportion and to ensure safety. There is a rule that says the height of each step added to the tread should equal 60 cm (24 in). A change of levels carefully managed, although ambitious, is an attractive feature in itself and could offer a retreat area at one end of the sunken herb garden. Hedges of lavender (*Lavandula*

· HANDY TIP ·

Use periwinkle (*Vinca major*) and its decorative forms to retain banks and sloping ground. Symbolically its binding quality is said to be enfolding in relationships and this applies to its stabilizing quality in the garden as well. A valuable evergreen for the labour-saving garden.

angustifolia) or rosemary (*Rosmarinus officinalis*) make fairly formal hedges to plant at each side of steps; and lemon balm (*Melissa officinalis*) placed at regular intervals would also emphasize the steps. If space allows, position containers filled with herbs at the side of each step, as these can be easily replaced or rearranged at will.

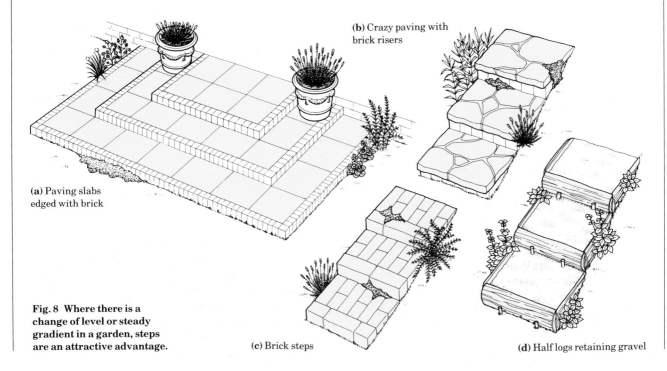

(b) Crazy paving with brick risers

(a) Paving slabs edged with brick

Fig. 8 Where there is a change of level or steady gradient in a garden, steps are an attractive advantage.

(c) Brick steps

(d) Half logs retaining gravel

ACQUIRING THE PLANTS

Ready to begin and full of ideas and good intentions for herb growing, the plants themselves now have to be acquired. Some may come as gifts from other herbalists, some will be purchased, many will be raised in pots or boxes or in nursery beds. All of them will be tiny plants that need constant care. So the first rule is not to acquire more than there is space for at the beginning; young plants, be they seedlings or rooted cuttings, should not be kept in pots or plastic pouches too long or they may perish.

How many plants will you need?

A fairly accurate assessment of the number of plants likely to be needed to plant up a given area is not difficult to calculate. All plants look better when planted together in groups of three, five or seven. Only so-called 'dot plants' or shrubs are planted singly.

- *Shrubby herbs* used to form edges to beds or borders need to be planted closely, about 30 cm (12 in) apart. Thus by measuring the distance round or along the bed, the number of young plants required can be calculated.

- *Hedge herbs* like lavender (*Lavandula angustifolia*), rosemary (*Rosmarinus officinalis*), sage (*Salvia officinalis*) and the apothecary's rose (*Rosa gallica officinalis*) should be put in as young plants and set 60-75 cm (24–30 in) apart.

- *Perennials* are planted 60–90 cm (24–36 in) apart, depending on their expected size when mature. Generally, majestic plants like lovage (*Levisticum officinale*), angelica (*Angelica archangelica*) and teasel (*Dipsacus fullonum*) need to be furthest apart and smaller ones like rue (*Ruta graveolens*) and lemon balm (*Melissa officinalis*) 60 cm (24 in) apart.

- *Creeping perennials* such as mint (*Mentha* species), chamomile (*Chamaemelum nobile*) and some carpet-rooting thymes (e.g. *Thymus herba-barona*) will soon cover a bed with only a few plants.

- *Annuals* can be spaced according to their ultimate size, although this can vary considerably from one season to the next and with soil and position. Try to give them a good start.

Buying plants

It is advisable to buy all the plants required for a herb garden scheme from the same source at the same time to ensure uniformity as the plants develop. But when there is time to establish the garden a few plants can be purchased and used as stock plants from which to propagate. The best plants to buy are those that are:

1. *Short noded* or bushy. A young plant that is weedy or etiolated (drawn) is never going to recover.

2. *Fresh* in appearance. Solid compost, perhaps with a greenish tinge to the surface, is not fresh and may have been overwatered.

3. *Upstanding* and devoid of roots creeping from the base of the pot.

4. *Labelled* with its correct name, so that an appropriate selection can be made.

Herb catalogues

Most herb nurseries produce good plant lists, some with helpful descriptions of the plants and advice on cultivation. It is sensible to become accustomed to the scientific names so that there is no confusion. Catalogues are of value, particularly when a collection of a given genus or type of plant is being assembled. They are invaluable also during winter evenings!

◄ A sheltered corner where marjorams, catmint, salvias and roses combine to form a pretty herb garden.

► Mop heads of angelica (*Angelica archangelica*) and cushions of lavender cotton (*Santolina* species) flank steps.

· 4 ·
Extending a Herb Garden

A dream herb garden is one where subtle colours and varying textures and lovely scents mingle on a calm summer evening. Shelter and a sense of security lent by a hedge or wall, or even provided by a trellis, add to the peace and enjoyment and offer a sense of retreat. A garden of such perfection may not be possible if you are a beginner but once a herb garden (however tiny) has been started, the realms of history, perfumery, culinary delights and aromatherapy are opened and become part of the atmosphere to stimulate further ideas for planting and garden design. The purpose of this chapter is to show how a basic theme for one herb garden can be developed and extended into something even more interesting. Gardening catalogues and herbals can provide a treasure-trove of ideas!

Developing formal designs

● *Extending a simple knot garden* A small knot garden, established in a couple of seasons, can be ideal as the central element in the design of a larger garden over the following two years, provided space allows. The plants (probably clipped) in the knot garden could be used in other free-growing ways around it, or the close-grown theme could form a surrounding border echoing the central knot in design. The border could take the form of a simple chain or block planting of the two or three dominant herbs in the knot. By repeating elements of the central design, a sense of continuity is maintained.

● *Extending a central knot or square plot* can be achieved by setting it in a circle which then in turn can be enriched in subsequent seasons. There is no need to try to create the whole garden at once; part of the enjoyment is in the development of ideas over a period of time.

● *Extending a central round bed* (Fig. 9) can also be effected by setting it in a square. The square should not be set too close to the central circle; the point is to *extend* the garden, not set it in a frame.

Where a central round bed is encircled by one or two larger beds, the temptation to develop the garden by adding further rings must be resisted. Try to break up existing rings or at regular intervals add dot plants such as standard honeysuckles (*Lonicera periclymenum*), or a bush of tree lupin (*Lupinus arboreus*), or make a wigwam on which summer jasmine (*Jasminum officinalis*) can swirl. In addition, try adding an archway to the outer circle to suggest entry to a special garden and make an arbour with a seat at one side. In outer beds add posts or arches over which the golden-leaved hop (*Humulus lupulus* 'Aureus') or sweet briar (*Rosa rubiginosa*) can scramble. The effect will only last through summer, but is well worth the effort.

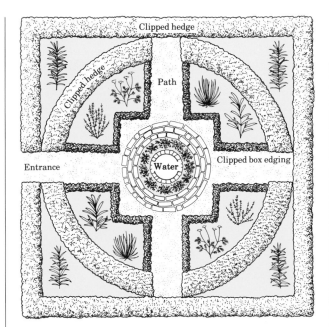

Fig. 9 Suggested layout for extending a small herb garden. A pattern of circles and squares works more successfully as a design than, for example, a series of concentric circles.

Developing informal designs

Where a herb border is filled with plants grown in a cottage-garden style, simple developments can be effective and sometimes lift the border from something prosaic to being far more special. The obvious extension would be to widen the border where space permits, be it a single-sided border backed by a building or hedge or a double-sided border. Realigning the edges, especially where they abut on to turf, to form curving bays, is another simple exercise. A few plants introduced into the interstices of a path alongside the border suggests that the garden is just drifting on and spreading like an incoming tide. This could offer the opportunity to use some pave and plant ideas (Fig. 3, page 18), using smaller paving stones or perhaps forming the squares in cobbles or bricks and setting them diamond fashion rather than square on to the border edge.

Variation through plant varieties

Whatever style the garden, the introduction of further varieties of plants is always eye-catching. If variegated or silver-leaved plants are added, place them to contrast other forms rather than together in a section. Golden or cream variegations when planted together and not relieved by other foliage can give a very colourless effect, especially in the early summer months when the foliage is fresh. It is in the selection of such plants that the purple-leaved and grey-leaved herbs assume greater importance as a foil. The bronze-purple leaves of the dark basil (*Ocimum basilicum* 'Dark Opal') and the purple plantain (*Plantago major* 'Rubrifolia') are both useful.

● *Some variegated and golden-leaved forms* of herbs to try are: ginger mint (*Mentha* × *gracilis* 'Variegata'), pine apple or apple mint (*M. suaveolens* 'Variegata'), the variegated lemon balm (*Melissa officinalis* 'Variegata'), and a golden-leaved form (*M.o.* 'Aurea') and the cultivar 'All Gold'. There are golden forms of meadowsweet (*Filipendula ulmaria* 'Aurea') and of marjoram (*Origanum* species). The latter vary enormously, sometimes reverting to green and sometimes displaying shoots tipped or suffused with gold. The cultivar *O. vulgare* 'Aureum Album' has gold leaves and white flowers. 'Gold Tip' has the point of each leaf painted yellow. The rue (*Ruta graveolens*) has a variegated form but it does not add much colour to the border and rue is best in its glaucous blue foliage of 'Jackman's Blue', and looks fine with the bronze fennel (*Foeniculum vulgare* var. *purpureum*). Then there is the golden sage (*Salvia officinalis* 'Icterina') which hugs the ground more than the grey-leaved plant and makes a good front-of-the-border feature, especially when mixed with the tricolor sage (*S.o.* 'Tricolor'), a daintier plant altogether.

39

▲ Clipped box (*Buxus sempervirens*) emphasizes an intricate formal open knot used as a potager where vegetables and herbs are grown side by side. Paving is used sympathetically to enhance the design.

▶ The value of variegated leaves is shown in this mixed planting of lavender 'Hidcote Blue', feverfew and painted sage.

● *Silver-leaved forms* add light and lift any planting arrangement. Among these herbs the artemisias rank high; their foliage is truly silver and not felted. Wormwood (*Artemisia absinthium* 'Lambrook Silver') has leaves that glisten and Roman wormwood (*Artemisia ponticum*) makes a froth of silver-grey because of a dense white down on both leaf surfaces; this is a good plant for the front of the border, but beware as it spreads quickly! Lavender cotton (*Santolina chamaecyparissus*) is almost white with downy leaves and the Neapolitan lavender cotton (*Santolina neapolitana*) has a taller and looser habit with more feathery foliage. Silver is found also in some thyme cultivars such as *Thymus* 'Silver Posie' and 'Silver Queen'. *Thymus lanuginosus* has grey leaves with a frosted effect.

● *Variations on flower colour* can also produce an eye-catching and interesting effect. While the true bergamot (*Monarda didyma*) has small red flowers, there are some good cultivars with various coloured flowers, e.g. 'Croftway Pink', a rich rose pink; 'Cambridge Scarlet', red and more brilliant than the type; 'Adam', ruby red; 'Snow Maiden', white; and 'Mahogany', a brownish red. The pale purple bobble heads of chives (*Allium shoenoprasm*) look most attractive when interplanted with the deep rose pink-flowered cultivar 'Forescate'.

Other herbs with an alternative flower colour to add interest to the garden are the lungworts (*Pulmonaria officinalis*) with a white and a red-flowered form, *alba* and *rubra*. Other pulmonarias do not look out of place among the herbs, but named cultivars do not derive from *officinalis*. So 'Mawson's Blue', 'Bowles' Red' and 'Munstead Blue' could each be tried. There is a white-flowered Jacob's ladder (*Polymonium caeruleum*) and cultivars with paler blue flowers.

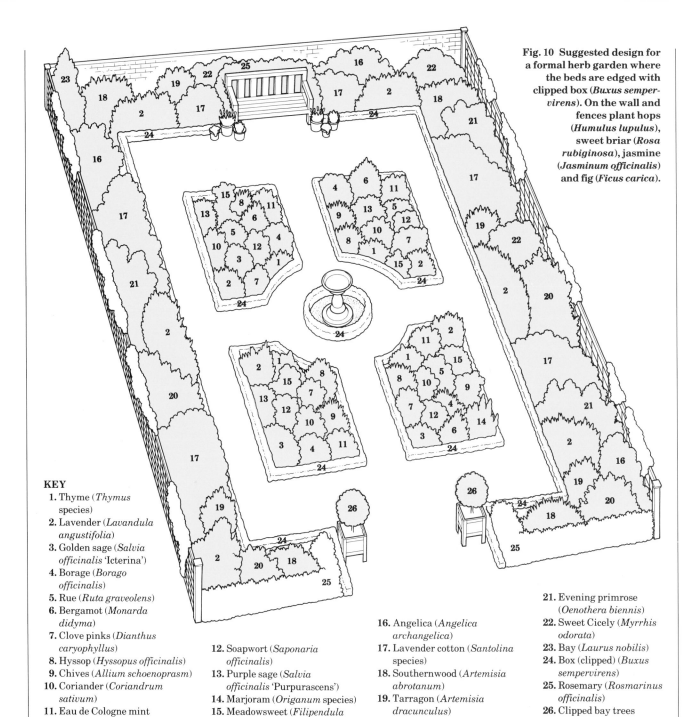

Fig. 10 Suggested design for a formal herb garden where the beds are edged with clipped box (*Buxus sempervirens*). On the wall and fences plant hops (*Humulus lupulus*), sweet briar (*Rosa rubiginosa*), jasmine (*Jasminum officinalis*) and fig (*Ficus carica*).

KEY

1. Thyme (*Thymus* species)
2. Lavender (*Lavandula angustifolia*)
3. Golden sage (*Salvia officinalis* 'Icterina')
4. Borage (*Borago officinalis*)
5. Rue (*Ruta graveolens*)
6. Bergamot (*Monarda didyma*)
7. Clove pinks (*Dianthus caryophyllus*)
8. Hyssop (*Hyssopus officinalis*)
9. Chives (*Allium schoenoprasm*)
10. Coriander (*Coriandrum sativum*)
11. Eau de Cologne mint (*Mentha × piperita citrata*)
12. Soapwort (*Saponaria officinalis*)
13. Purple sage (*Salvia officinalis* 'Purpurascens')
14. Marjoram (*Origanum* species)
15. Meadowsweet (*Filipendula ulmaria*)
16. Angelica (*Angelica archangelica*)
17. Lavender cotton (*Santolina* species)
18. Southernwood (*Artemisia abrotanum*)
19. Tarragon (*Artemisia dracunculus*)
20. Fennel (*Foeniculum vulgare*)
21. Evening primrose (*Oenothera biennis*)
22. Sweet Cicely (*Myrrhis odorata*)
23. Bay (*Laurus nobilis*)
24. Box (clipped) (*Buxus sempervirens*)
25. Rosemary (*Rosmarinus officinalis*)
26. Clipped bay trees (*Laurus nobilis*)

42

Growing herbs with other plants

The choice of plants for a herb garden is a personal one but for other scented plants to lend an air of a country garden amass with traditional plants where bees and butterflies might hover, here are some suitable suggestions.

● *Roses* always spring to mind for the scented garden and the best to choose for fragrance are the old bush roses. There are four main kinds: Damask, Centifolia, Bourbons and Gallica roses. The latter are perhaps the oldest of all garden roses and are believed to have originated more than a thousand years BC.

The Damasks are rather lax shrubs, elegant in habit and forming quite airy bushes. *R.* 'Comte de Chambord' is one to try for smaller gardens with its bright pink flowers on and off throughout the season. A particularly fragrant one, where there is more space, is 'La Ville de Bruxelles', with really big rich pink flowers that weigh the branches down to give an air of abundance.

Centifolias are very thorny and usually the flowers are a true 'cabbage' shape with petals crammed in the centre of the flower, and frequently they hang their heads. They are high on the list for richness of fragrance. A low-growing one is 'De Meaux', which was first grown in the late eighteenth century, with smaller flowers of pure pink, supported by rather twiggy growth. A larger one is the paler pink 'Fantin Latour', whose petals sometimes fold back at the edge.

Bourbon roses strongly resemble more modern garden roses but carry the deep, rich, true rose scent of the old roses. The flowers are heavy and velvety. 'Boule de Neige', as its name suggests, is a good white rose with flowers carried in clusters amid dark foliage. 'Honorine de Brabant' has pale pink flowers painted with raspberry red freckles and stripes and evokes that fruit in its scent.

Above all it is the Gallica roses that belong in the herb garden, being the descendents of the old apothecary's rose (*Rosa gallica officinalis*). Rich shades of red from crimson through to purple are

---

· HERBS WITH SCENTED AND TEXTURED LEAVES ·

These can be particularly enjoyed by the partially sighted.

Name	Leaf description
Angelica (*Angelica archangelica*)	Large, shiny, aromatic
Bay (*Laurus nobilis*)	Tough, pungent when broken
Bergamot (*Monarda didyma*)	Soft, sweetly aromatic of orange
Feverfew (*Tanacetum parthenium*)	Elaborately cut and shaped; aromatic
Hyssop (*Hyssopus officinalis*)	Spiky, tough, pungent
Juniper (*Juniperus communis*)	Tough, stringy, camphorus
Lavender (*Lavandula angustifolia*)	Small, roughish, aromatic
Lavender cotton (*Santolina* species)	Cord-like, pungent, some soft and oily
Lemon balm (*Melissa officinalis*)	Rough, blistery, strongly aromatic of lemon
Lemon verbena (*Aloysia triphylla*)	Thin, smooth, strongly aromatic of lemon
Marigold (*Calendula officinalis*)	Slightly rough form, pungent
Mints (*Mentha* species)	Firm, sharp, minty aroma
Parsley (*Petroselinum crispum*)	Curled; clean aroma
Rosemary (*Rosmarinus officinalis*)	Spiky, oily, scented
Rue (*Ruta graveolens*)	Soft, fragmented; odour of stale orange
Sage (*Salvia officinalis*)	Rough, dry, firm, pungent
Southernwood (*Artemisia abrotanum*)	Very soft, feathery, sweetly camphorous
Sweet Cicely (*Myrrhis odorata*)	Large, soft, fresh, downy and lacy
Tansy (*Tanacetum vulgare*)	Firm, much indented, pungent
Thyme (*Thymus* species)	Small, twiggy, aromatic, somewhat camphorous

displayed by these roses on small shrubs. If there is room for only one rose in the herb garden it has to be this one, or its form *R. versicolor*, 'Rosa Mundi', a striking striped pink and red.

For pot-pourri all these old roses are the ones to use for their rich and true rose scent. Catalogues will give details of many more old bush roses.

● *Other fragrant plants* from which to choose include some cottage plants like dames violet (*Hesperis matrionalis*), wallflowers (*Erysimum cheiri*) and other erysimums such as the popular 'Bowles' Mauve'. Clove pink (*Dianthus caryophyllus*), mignonette (*Reseda odorata*), the tobacco plant (*Nicotiana alata*) and peonies also have their place.

The red-flowered peony (*Paeonia officinalis*) is an ancient herb, but more elegant cultivars could

· HANDY TIP ·

Some shrubs can be planted in the herb garden (see below). However, do not try to grow herbs in the shrub border. There will be insufficient light and moisture so that ultimately the plants will not carry the rich aromas.

be included in this garden for their freshness and sophistication.

● *Shrubs* with scented flowers, where there is room, could include lilacs, and two low-growing ones (*Syringa* × *persica*) with lilac blue flowers, thought to have been grown in England since the mid-seventeenth century; and *S. microphylla* with rose-mauve flowers, would be a suitable choice. Elder (*Sambucus nigra*) and its various forms such as the golden-leaved fern elder (*S.n. lacinata aurea*) is another genus to include legitimately for elder flowers and berries, and provided innumerable remedies and flavours for our great grandmothers. The curry plant (*Helichrysum angustifolium*, also known as *H. italicum*) with its hot curry supper aroma, lights up a corner with its almost metallic silver foliage, and the Mexican orange blossom (*Choisya ternata*) is especially buoyant in its golden-leaved form 'Aurea'. The Spanish broom (*Spartium junceum*), with its sprays of fragrant yellow pea-flowers on arching growth, can be kept in shape by cutting back regularly.

Another lovely little shrub is the tree lupin (*Lupinus arboreus*) which grows quickly but is a short-lived plant, wonderful for its vanilla scent.

▶ **A small bed of herbs often associates well with roses and other plants.**

· HERBS THAT ATTRACT BEES ·	
Name	**Flower colour**
Anise hyssop (*Agastache foeniculum*)	Mauve
Bay (*Laurus nobilis*)	Cream
Borage (*Borago officinalis*)	Blue
Box (*Buxus sempervirens*)	Cream
Chicory (*Cichorium intybus*)	Blue
Chives (*Allium schoenoprasm*)	Mauve
Evening primrose (*Oenothera biennis*)	Yellow
Horehound, white (*Marrubium vulgare*)	White
Jacob's ladder (*Polemoniun caeruleum*)	Blue
Lavender (*Lavandula* species and cultivars)	Mauve
Lungwort (*Pulmonaria officinalis*)	Blue/pink
Marjoram (*Origanum* species)	Pink
Mint (*Mentha* species)	Mauve
Mullein (*Verbascum thapsus*)	Yellow
Rosemary (*Rosmarinus officinalis*)	Pale blue
Sage (*Salvia officinalis*)	Mauve
Savory (*Satureia* species)	White
Sea holly (*Eryngium maritima*)	Pale blue
Thyme (*Thymus* species)	Mauve/pink
Yarrow (*Achillea millefolium*)	White

· 5 ·

Decorative Herb Features

While one of the first thoughts you may have towards trying something different in the herb garden is to raise the aroma nearer to nose level, it is not until the end of the first season that you realize how full and tall some herbs become. Consider ways in which the scents and lovely aromatic leaves can be enjoyed by getting some plants to shoulder level, if not higher. Various suggestions are in this chapter, together with other popular ideas for ways of enjoying growing herbs.

ELEVATED IDEAS (Fig. 11)

Arches

Arches are universally popular but frequently fail to achieve their ideal because they are not sited correctly. They have to serve a more important purpose than simply to bear the weight of plants and need to be placed where they announce the entrance to the herb garden, perhaps with a border or trellis on either side, or put where they can frame a view or focal point such as a seat or sundial.

Pergolas and loggias

These can be formed by three or four arches together. They can be constructed from a variety of materials to complement the house or the ambience of the garden. Set against the house wall or herb garden wall, either would form a pleasant place to sit out in. A collection of herbs growing in pots could be placed at the base of each post and climbers allowed to scale the heights.

Raised beds

Raised beds are invaluable for the disabled gardener. The soil level can be brought up to 60–70 cm (24–28 in), or any convenient height. Such beds have been called 'billiard tables' which they can rather resemble. They need to be stoutly constructed, with walls built of brick or stone, or made from old railway sleepers or similar material. Ideally a raised bed in which herbs are to grow should be an island bed, allowing access all around it.

Shelter is absolutely essential for the setting of the bed. By the time one or two tall-growing herbs are established, a stiff breeze could ruin the entire display.

● *Method* Rubble and hardcore are put in the base and topped with garden top soil. Where herbs are to be cultivated, leave the surface fairly level. The bed will need to be prepared as for borders in the open garden, and the same routine followed throughout the year. Any herb that accepts the situation as far as light and shade are concerned can be cultivated, and to give a decorative air it is a good idea to keep the smaller plants at the front and sides of the bed. This will also make it easier to care for the plants in the centre.

For the front of the bed, look for plants which will fall forward to blur the outline of the bricks. Some suggestions are: chives (*Allium schoenoprasm*), wall germander (*Teucrium chamaedrys*), caraway (*Carum carvi*), violets and heartsease (*Viola* species), thymes (*Thymus* species), parsley (*Petroselinum crispum*), pinks (*Dianthus caryophyllus*), feverfew (*Tanacetum parthenium*) and marjorams (*Origanum* species).

HERBS IN CONTAINERS

Herbs, like numerous other plants, can be grown in containers for display. Pots, boxes, tubs, ornamental troughs or jars can all be used, as can unconventional receptacles such as cooking pots, hay baskets and wheelbarrows. Receptacles other than flower pots must have holes bored in the base for the purpose of drainage. Herein lies the fun of growing herbs, for the range of plants can be broadened perhaps to include tender plants, or those that the local climate would not support normally.

Container-grown plants are the most versatile asset in the imaginative herb garden. Pots can be assembled to focus interest, even as a central feature, or be moved into borders to create colour contrast or merely fill a gap in flowering, set astride walls, flank a flight of steps or punctuate the edge of a terrace or balcony.

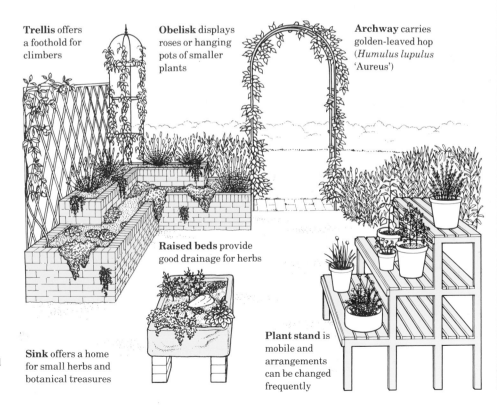

Trellis offers a foothold for climbers

Obelisk displays roses or hanging pots of smaller plants

Archway carries golden-leaved hop (*Humulus lupulus* 'Aureus')

Raised beds provide good drainage for herbs

Sink offers a home for small herbs and botanical treasures

Plant stand is mobile and arrangements can be changed frequently

Fig. 11 Various features provide additional planting space for small gardens, and can be managed by the infirm gardener.

Management of containers

The correct proportion of the mature plant to its container has to be considered, and is vital for success.

Cleaning the inside of containers is important prior to planting. Terracotta pots need to be soaked in water for a few hours before being planted up.

Composts can be based upon John Innes No. 2, sometimes adding peat or coir to encourage moisture retention, or grit to ensure drainage. An adequate amount of drainage material (crocks, grit, bark chippings, gravel, etc) needs to be placed in the base of the pot before filling up with soil. Plants will not survive in waterlogged airless compost.

▲ Where space is at a premium, or even without a garden, a collection of culinary herbs can be made in pots.

► Containers and a wheelbarrow filled with pots of parsley, bay, lavender, sorrel, rosemary and chives.

Pot up in spring or sow seed and thin to the strongest seedlings a little later.

Groups of plants can be assembled into one large container; each plant should have roughly the same amount of compost as if in a smaller individual pot. Colour and leaf form provide the foil for one plant to another. Perhaps a grey leaf like sage (*Salvia officinalis*) against the blue grey of rue (*Ruta graveolens*) or painted sage (*S.o.* 'Tricolor') with lavenders and chives. Foliage plants and those with definite flowers are generally more successful. Large herbs such as angelica (*Angelica archangelica*) and lovage (*Levisticum officinale*) or elecampane (*Inula helenium*) are better in the border, although the foliage of fennel is useful.

Watering is a daily routine for container-grown plants, taking the weather into account. Shallow bowls will require more frequent watering than deeper ones.

Feed regularly with a proprietary liquid plant food through the summer. Foliar feeding helps also as daily watering tends to leach (wash away) plant nutrients from compost and the roots cannot forage for food elsewhere. The plants must be nurtured.

Dead-head during the summer to stimulate further flower growth – after all, the herbs are in pots for decorative purposes. Seeds can be allowed to form late in the season.

Protect pots through winter, but it is more exciting to replant the whole assemblage each summer.

Large containers

In very large containers such as stone bowls or cattle drinking troughs, it is best to either bury pots in compost, bark chippings or pebbles or plant rooted cuttings so that you can easily replace them if they grow out of proportion with

the general arrangement. Even when potted plants are used in this way, adequate drainage holes are needed in the base and sides of the container.

• *A strawberry barrel* can look most attractive when planted up with herbs. The size of the mature plants in relation to the pot and to one another needs to be taken into consideration. Plants like wild strawberry (*Fragaria vesca*), painted sage (*Salvia officinalis* 'Tricolor'), golden sage (*S.o.* 'Icterina'), buckler-leaved sorrel (*Rumex scutatus*) and savory (*Satureia hortensis*) look particularly lovely in such a pot. To pot up the compost needs to be added in layers and the young plants pushed through the holes at different levels to lie on the compost before another layer is put in. The top of the container is planted up in the normal way. As the work proceeds, insert a couple of narrow tubes (piping), long enough to reach to the lower levels of the compost. This will ensure that water reaches the lower plants, rather than immediately running away through the planting holes.

• *A stone sink* offers the opportunity to make a small herb garden. Fill it with a collection of thymes (*Thymus* species) or with several small herbs such as houseleek (*Sempervirens tectorum*), salad burnet (*Sanguisorba minor*), parsley (*Petroselinum crispum*), small lavenders such as *Lavandula angustifolia* 'Hidcote', violets (*Viola* species), wild strawberry (*Fragaria vesca*), rock hyssop (*Hyssopus officinalis aristatus*), clove pinks (*Dianthus caryophyllus*) and lady's mantle (*Alchemilla vulgaris*).

Window boxes

Window boxes, or flower boxes as they are known in the U.S., are invaluable for balconies, in porches, to edge a terrace, along a low wall or on a flat roof. Whatever material forms the box, it can either be planted up direct or filled with purpose-made smaller baskets which are themselves planted and can be removed and exchanged easily as the seasons change. Such baskets are an asset as they are light even when planted and can be moved more easily than the window box, even by disabled gardeners. On a wooden staging such as can be constructed by a do-it-yourself enthusiast, flower boxes can make a remarkably attractive display and are easier to manage than a series of pots would be on the staging.

The cultural procedure is the same as for all containers, with careful attention being given to the most important operations of watering, weeding and deadheading.

· HERBS TO GROW IN WINDOW BOXES ·

Basil, purple (*Osimum basilicum* 'Dark Opal')

Box (*Buxus sempervirens*)

Catnip (*Nepeta catarica*)

Chamomile (flowering) (*Chamaemelum nobile*)

Chives
• mauve-flowered (*Allium schoenoprasm*)
• pink-flowered (*A.s* 'Forescate')

Geranium (scented leaved) (*Pelargonium* species)

Lavender
• French (*Lavandula stoechas*)
• low-growing (*Lavandula angustifolia* cultivars)
• white (*L.a.* 'Nana Alba')

Lavender cotton (*Santolina* species)

Lemon balm (*Melissa officinalis*)

Lungwort (*Pulmonaria officinalis*)

Marigold (*Calendula officinalis*)

Marjoram (*Origanum* species)

Mint
• apple (*Mentha suaveolens* 'Variegata')
• ginger (*M.* × *gracilis*)

Rue (*Ruta graveolens*)

Sage
• golden (*Salvia officinalis* 'Icterina')
• painted (*S.o.* 'Tricolor')
• purple (*S.o.* 'Purpurascens')

Soapwort (*Saponaria officianlis*)

Tarragon (*Artemisia dracunculus*)

Thyme (*Thymus vulgaris*)

Violets (*Viola* species)

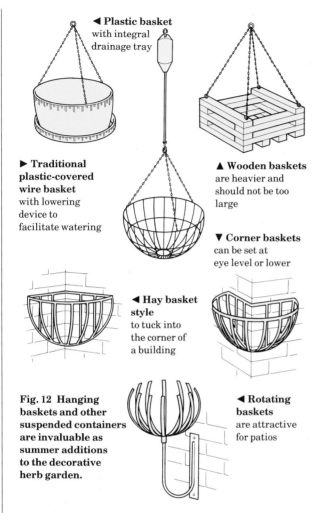

◀ **Plastic basket**
with integral
drainage tray

▶ **Traditional
plastic-covered
wire basket**
with lowering
device to
facilitate watering

▲ **Wooden baskets**
are heavier and
should not be too
large

▼ **Corner baskets**
can be set at
eye level or lower

◀ **Hay basket
style**
to tuck into
the corner of
a building

**Fig. 12 Hanging
baskets and other
suspended containers
are invaluable as
summer additions
to the decorative
herb garden.**

◀ **Rotating
baskets**
are attractive
for patios

Herb baskets (Fig. 12)

One of the primary decorative additions to any property, domestic or commercial, is a hanging basket – a plant container designed to be suspended above head height. Some herbs can be cultivated for the summer months in this way, although it has to be said that the overall effect is less showy than the striking bedding plants habitually displayed in baskets.

Manufacturers now offer hanging baskets in both metal and plastic that will tuck into a corner or wrap around a corner, or fit around the gutter downpipe. A recent innovation is a swivelling basket which can be attached to walls or fences or gateposts, or any upright stable structure. Garden centres also offer elaborate frames that carry four or five hanging baskets as a decorative feature that can be moved round the garden.

Planting has to be done with great care in early summer, packing in plants slightly more closely than for other types of container. Stand the basket on a bucket or box to do the work. A water-retaining lining is first spread inside the basket, or a layer of sphagnum moss followed by a sheet of green plastic (such as garden refuse bags are made from), into which drainage holes have been punched. Use compost such as John Innes No. 2. Tuck in the plants as the basket is filled, and push them into the sides of the basket. Set trailing ones at the edges to hang over.

Watering is of paramount importance and some baskets will need to be attended to three times a day during warm or windy weather, because the ratio of soil to plant is quite unsatisfactory for a happy existence. To avoid too much splashing on the ground beneath the basket, watering ought to be done slowly, although when containers are aloft this is difficult to carry out. Baskets can sometimes be watered with ice cubes if these are available. They melt slowly and the water is more readily retained by the compost.

● *Herb basket plants* should include those with graceful stems such as periwinkle (*Vinca major*), best in its variegated form *V.m.* 'Variegata', but either will tolerate shade, along with some of the mints (*Mentha* species). Mints to tuck into the sides of the baskets include ginger mint (*M × gracilis*) and the variegated apple mint (*M. suaveolens* 'Variegata').Thymes are useful also, *T. vulgaris* and *T. herba barona* being the best. The

spotted dead nettle (*Lamium maculatum*) has several decorative forms like the cultivars 'Gold Nuggets' with golden leaves, and 'Pink Pewter' with metallic silver leaves and pink flowers which will trail down from the basket. Other suggestions to include are chives (*Allium schoenoprasm*), parsley (*Petroselinum crispum*), ivy (*Hedera helix*), lady's mantle (*Alchemilla vulgaris*) and rooted cuttings of rosemary (*Rosmarinus officinalis*) and rue (*Ruta graveolens*).

HERB LAWNS

The first alternative to turf that most gardeners consider is chamomile (*Chamaemelum nobile*). However, to make a chamomile lawn and maintain it may sound romantic and nostalgic, but unless time can be devoted to it in the early stages, the exercise may prove to be somewhat disappointing. Other herbs such as thyme (*Thymus* species) are equally useful, possibly more so, except that the resulting growth is a carpeting mass, uneven in surface, but scented and spongey to walk on: the image of 'lawn' has to be revised.

Making a chamomile lawn or pathway

Chamomile (*Chamaemelum nobile*) produces a fairly hardwearing surface of apple-scented feathery foliage of an unvaried mid-pale green. It will never feel as firm as a grass turf.
1. Prepare the area thoroughly. Time spent on levelling and clearing every trace of perennial weed is the secret behind a successful herb lawn.
2. Remove about 5 cm (2 in) of top soil, level and add a 2.5–5 cm (1–2 in) layer of potting grit as an underlay.
3. Return the top soil, rake and level.
4. Add compost or a sprinkling of an organic fertilizer such as bonemeal or dried blood, and rake in.

◀ **A chamomile path flanked by massed flowers of fennel in a sheltered herb garden.**

▲ **A chamomile lawn composed of *Chamaemelum nobile* 'Treneague'.**

5. Roll and firm the whole area to ensure a good tilth and even surface.
6. *Chamaemelum nobile* seed can be sown in spring and the weaker seedlings thinned out later to about 10 cm (4 in) apart. Alternatively, set out plantlets at 10 cm (4 in) apart both ways in staggered rows (so that the diagonal row runs across the area).
7. Plant a few surplus plants in a nursery border.
8. Water in and hand weed with care for the following summer. If the soil is wet after rain, use

53

boards to stand on while you carry out the work.

9. Replace failed plants or fill bare patches with plants from the nursery bed.

10. Roll and trim with shears as required. Dress with lawn sand in the autumn.

11. A well-established lawn can be mown in subsequent summers, with the blades set high.

Making a thyme lawn or bank

To make a thyme lawn the basic requirements and procedures are the same as for a chamomile lawn except that a selection of thymes (*Thymus serpyllum*) should be used together in little groups. It is therefore necessary to form a sward from small plants.

1. Allow five plants of each species or cultivar to form each group and plant them irregularly, not in rows, setting them 15 cm (6 in) apart. This will ensure an even marbled effect over the area when the plants are in flower.

2. Contrasting leaf colours need to be included so that when the plants are not in bloom a pretty dappled effect can be achieved. The whole patch should be very decorative.

3. Maintenance includes hand weeding, especially in the early days, and filling in any bare patches that occur.

4. Cut back in late summer after flowering with hand clippers to encourage fresh shoot formation and to ensure close carpeting.

Aromatic walkways and driveways.

A few aromatic plants like chamomile and thyme seem not to suffer from being crushed by passing feet; some thymes (*Thymus* species) will even tolerate a car being driven over them occasionally. On paved areas such as drives, patios and swimming pool surrounds plants will thrive when tucked between paving stones to break up the level surface. Some paving stones can be removed

---

· HANDY HINT ·

When planting chamomile to make a path or lawn or setting it between stepping stones, use the non-flowering kind, *Chamaemelum nobile* 'Treneague'. Not only does it save work because there's no dead-heading to be done, but the green sward is of a better appearance throughout the season.

---

in order to plant something in the small soil space. The golden rule is to maintain the proportions between area and plant. For instance it would be inadvisable to plant angelica (*Angelica archangelica*) or lovage (*Levisticum officinale*) in a small area. The plants ought to be introduced with discretion, dotting them about to give the impression that they have seeded themselves, and in no way form a block to prevent easy progress along the drive. Herbs to introduce in this way include houseleek (*Sempervivum tectorum*), lavender cotton (*Santolina* species), lady's mantle (*Alchemilla vulgaris*), pinks (*Dianthus caryophyllus*), and feverfew (*Tanacetum parthenium*). *Thymus vulgaris* and its forms are hummock or cushion forming; all other thymes flow over the stones, making flowered pools.

· HERBS FOR LAWNS AND PATHS ·

For sun
Chamomile
(*Chamaemelum nobile*)
Ground ivy (*Glechoma hederacea*)
Purple-leaved plantain
(*Plantago major* 'Rubrifolia')

Salad burnet (*Sanguisorba minor*)
Thyme (*Thymus serpyllum*)
Yarrow (*Achillea millefolium*)
For shade
Pennyroyal (*Mentha pulegium*)

SEATS

A herb bench (Fig. 13)

Traditionally a herb bench is formed with fruit-scented chamomile (*Chamaemelum nobile*) used to form either the 'cushion' of the seat or, when the seat itself is set in a bank, to form the 'arms' and cover the bank behind. Preparation and maintenance are the same as for a chamomile lawn (see page 53), though the smaller area is often quicker to establish and easier to maintain. Select the non-flowering *C.n.* 'Treneague'. Thymes can be planted in the bank mixed in with the chamomile to enhance the scented area, but be aware that thyme attracts bees. Aromatic and scented herbs can be planted between the paving stones at the foot of the seat. Suitable ones are: low-growing lavenders (*Lavandula* cultivars), clove pink (*Dianthus caryophyllus*), wild strawberry (*Fragaria vesca*), woodruff (*Galium odoratum*) in shade, salad burnet (*Sanguisorba officinalis*) and marjorams (*Origanum* species).

Where space allows, the bench could be extended to form one end of the garden, or herbs in containers arranged close at hand so that the flowers and scents can be enjoyed. Raised beds

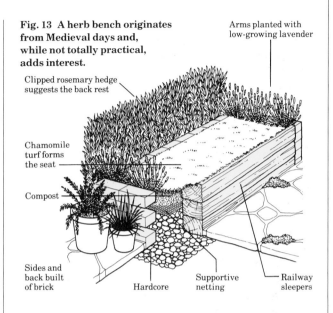

Fig. 13 A herb bench originates from Medieval days and, while not totally practical, adds interest.

Arms planted with low-growing lavender

Clipped rosemary hedge suggests the back rest

Chamomile turf forms the seat

Compost

Sides and back built of brick

Hardcore

Supportive netting

Railway sleepers

could be constructed of either mellow brick or stone to form the 'sides' of the bench and planted up with treasured plants to be enjoyed at eye and nose level. The happiest way to keep the selection fresh is to replant it each alternate year to prevent legginess which would allow the plants to fall about and restrict the sitting space. Or pots could be sunk into the raised bed and the surface covered with bark chippings or pebbles to act as a mulch in addition to giving a neat effect. Plants to choose for the sides of the seat are: wall germander (*Teucrium chamaedrys*), hyssop (*Hyssopus officinalis*), clove pink (*Dianthus caryophyllus*), the painted-leaved mints such as ginger mint (*Mentha × gracilis*) and the variegated apple mint (*Mentha suaveolens* 'Variegata').

A bench arbour

A practical seat is an essential feature of a herb garden on which to relax and enjoy the haze of colour and perfumes. A simple design can be

---

· COLONIZING HERBS FOR GROUND COVER ·

Bistort (*Polygonum bistorta*)	Lavender (*Lavandula angustifolia*)
Chamomile (*Chamaemelum nobile*)	Lungwort (*Pulmonaria officinalis*)
Evening primrose (*Oenothera biennis*)	Rosemary (*Rosmarinus officinalis*)
Ground ivy (*Glechoma hederacea*)	Spotted dead nettle (*Lamium maculatum*)
Hyssop (*Hyssopus officinalis*)	Thyme (*Thymus serpyllum*)
Juniper (*Juniperus communis*)	Woodruff (*Galium odorata*)
	Yarrow (*Achillea millefolium*)

stained or painted to blend in with the garden and will provide support for climbing and scrambling herbs. Plants can be grown in large containers or planted nearby.

● *Climbing plants* have a tendency to stretch upwards to the heights and become bare at the base. Tall herbs can be planted to accompany them to clothe the lower parts of posts and supports. Try fennel (*Foeniculum vulgare*), angelica (*Angelica archangelica*), lovage (*Levisticum officinale*), and elecampane (*Inula helenium*).

● *Scented plants* to use for an arbour or supports include summer jasmine (*Jasminum officinalis*) for its dainty dark leaves and very fragrant white flowers, although it is unlikely to thrive in cold districts. Virgin's bower (*Clematis recta*) is a perennial scrambler which will need to be tied in one or two places as the season progresses. The small sweetly scented white flowers in summer are upstanding away from the leaves. Discourage children and hay fever sufferers from playing with the foliage, as it causes irritation to the eyes. Honeysuckle (*Lonicera periclymenum*), which the

Carpeting thyme flows over the gravel at the foot of a wooden seat enfolded in catmint.

Golden hops (*Humulus lupulus*) unfurl on posts in this spacious potager-style garden.

herbalist John Gerard claimed 'removeth wearisomeness . . . and hicket' (hiccough), will twine its way over an arbour quickly and produce heavily scented flowers of pink and cream in high summer. Honeysuckle attracts moths in the evening, so may not be everyone's choice for a restful spot in the garden. Unfortunately, it also looks very dismal in winter when the leaves fall and the twisted stems look like writhing ropes. Passion flowers (*Passiflora* species) are cultivated for their curiously attractive flowers and some edible fruit. The herb passion vine (*P. incarnata*) dies back in winter and produces very sweetly scented cream flowers tinged with purple in summer. They must all be treated as tender vigorous climbers.

● *Foliage plants* suitable for arbours and supports include: the golden-leaved hop (*Humulus lupulus* 'Aureus') which quickly produces lashes of rich growth with vine-like leaves. Grow a female plant as this is the one that bears the aromatic papery cones in late summer.

Ivy (*Hedera helix*) is available in a whole range of decorative-leaved forms, many of them dainty. It is a poisonous evergreen that does not flower until it reaches the summit of its support, however tall. The vine (*Vitis vinifera*) has long been used for the medical action of its sugar and can be found in numerous coloured-leaved forms. All of them have a graceful habit of decorating a support with flowing long young growths.

OTHER FEATURES

A herb ladder (Fig. 14)

Where there is no space at all in which to cultivate a few herbs, shelves could be attached to a wall and pots or bowls of herbs accommodated on them. Obviously a careful arrangement of shelves sufficiently far apart will be more effective than a tier of 'bookshelves'.

Make a series of troughs rather than shelves on any wall other than a north-facing one. The general effect is that of a ladder, and the supporting sides can be upright or lean inwards symmetrically to suggest an arch or tent. Use stout boards at least 40 cm (15 in) wide for the sides and attach them firmly to the wall. Individual troughs are constructed by a board about 25–40 cm (10–15 in) long, being attached to the supports and inclined at the lower edge towards the wall. A total height of about 3 m (10 ft) looks most effective and gives ten tiers.

It is a good idea to drill one or two holes low down on each plank, in different positions at each level to help drainage without forming channels that run downwards. Scatter grit or aggregate to a depth of about 8 cm (3 in) in the base of each little triangular trough and fill up with a suitable growing media.

Plant up in the spring or early summer and when the young plants begin to settle in, add a few pretty stones to the soil surface to act as a mulch and to enhance the ladder's appearance.

Smaller or compact plants are the most successful grown in this way, and certainly the most effective. Plants that are too large will fall forward and spoil the effect of the 'wall of plants'. Plants to choose are: houseleek (*Sempervivum tectorum*), thymes (*Thymus* species), Heartsease and violets (*Viola* species), small lavenders (*Lavandula* cultivars), salad burnet (*Sanguisorba minor*), cowslip (*Primula veris*), wild strawberry (*Fragaria vesca*), chamomile (*Chamaemelum nobile*), painted sage (*Salvia officinalis* 'Tricolor'), wall germander (*Teucrium chamaedrys*), lungwort (*Pulmonaria officinalis*), bistort (*Polygonum bistorta*) and woodruff (*Asperula odorata*).

Introduce rooted cuttings as for container-grown arrangements and change them when they grow too big. This way some of the following plants can be included in the ladder, if only seasonally: Rosemary (*Rosmarinus officinalis*), lavender cotton (*Santolina* species), rue (*Ruta graveolens*), lavender (*Lavandula angustifolia*), hyssop (*Hyssopus officinalis*), winter savory (*Satureia montana*).

A ladder on the ground
The pattern and theme of 'steps' can be created on the ground as an edging to a path or perhaps down one side of a long narrow garden. One herb is grown in a small bed about 60 cm (24 in) by 45 cm (18 in), then an equal area of turf or paving material is set end on, narrow edges adjacent, followed by another bed of equal dimensions for a single herb, and so on. If the whole area is outlined by boards or bricks or logs, the pattern

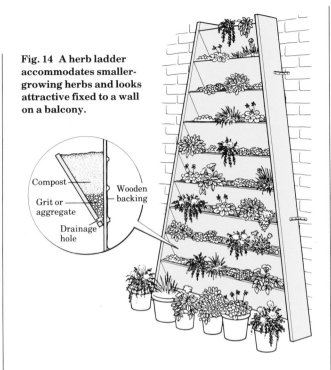

Fig. 14 A herb ladder accommodates smaller-growing herbs and looks attractive fixed to a wall on a balcony.

Compost

Grit or aggregate

Wooden backing

Drainage hole

resembles a ladder. For effectiveness select the lower-growing herbs and leave out the taller ones from the scheme. Such a block pattern is really only suited to an area where it can be looked down upon from the windows of the house or from a terrace.

A 'ladder' of this kind can be set along either side of a path and constitute a herb garden in itself. The same idea could be translated to form the perimeter bed of a formal herb garden, when for impact a repetitive planting theme should be introduced. Try evening primrose (*Oenothera biennis*) alternating with various mints (*Mentha* species) and these contained beds would be ideal for restraining the wandering roots.

Potager
Jardin potager is the French for 'kitchen garden' and has come to be used colloquially to describe a garden wherein vegetables, fruit and herbs are

cultivated, laid out ornamentally. Often beds are edged with low formal hedges, or seasonally with ornamental vegetables such as carnival-coloured cabbages or red orach (*Atriplex hortensis* var. *rubra*). A potager is highly suited to urban areas where land is at a premium and where a whole range of herbs find a rightful place alongside modern compact fruit tree forms, cottage flowers for cutting and the vegetables which contemporary gardeners no longer grow in rows. A simple design of rectangular beds will suffice, or paths may radiate from a central point or from a seat at one side or from a terrace.

Where herbs are mixed in with fruit and vegetables the same cultural requirements regarding light and shade and soil apply.

Herbs for the waterside

Once the herbs are established denizens of a garden it is always tempting to see in which location, other than the herb garden proper, they will grow. Water gardens are increasingly popular and there is no reason to think that herbs do not have a role to play there.

All the mints, with the exception of apple mint (*Mentha suaveolens* 'Variegata'), like damp conditions and especially the water mint (*Mentha aquatica*), as its name suggests. The yellow-flowered iris (*Iris pseudacorus*) is a natural choice as it is found in the wild on river banks. Meadowsweet (*Filipendula ulmaria*), comfrey (*Symphytum officinale*) and sweet rush (*Acorus calamus*) love water margins. The latter has orange-scented leaves.

GROWING HERBS INDOORS

To have fresh herbs for use all year round represents an ideal for many cooks. With a little more care than the plants need for outdoor

Companion planting

Companion planting is a cult, founded upon a little folk-lore together with some research that has been conducted by one or two serious organizations with varying conclusions. It embodies a down-to-earth, environmentally friendly approach that despite natural discrepencies of soil, rainfall and humidity, claims that some plants are companionable to one another, others antagonistic. To plant together certain companionable plants can be of mutual benefit, even acting as a natural deterrent for insect pests. There is still a great deal to be confirmed about plant scents and root excretions, but companion planting is well worth trying out for yourself.

Herbs and their companions

Herb	Companion
Angelica (*Angelica archangelica*)	Parsley
Basil (*Ocimum basilicum*)	Parsley, tomatoes
Bergamot (*Monarda didyma*)	Cabbage family
Caraway (*Carum carvi*)	Cabbage family
Chamomile (*Chamaemelum nobile*)	Cabbage family
Chives (*Allium shoenoprasm*)	Carrots
Hyssop (*Hyssopus officinalis*)	Cabbage family
Lavender (*Lavandula angustifolia*)	Potatoes
Lemon balm (*Melissa officinalis*)	Potatoes, tomatoes
Marjoram (*Origanum* species)	Potatoes, beans
Mint (*Mentha* species)	Potatoes, cabbage family
Rosemary (*Rosmarinus officinalis*)	Beans, cabbage, carrots
Southernwood (*Artemisia abrotanum*)	Fruit trees
Tansy (*Tanacetum vulgare*)	Fruit trees and roses
Thyme (*Thymus* species)	Cabbage family, broad beans

An extensive vegetable garden with herbs rosemary, lavender and ruby chard growing side by side.

cultivation, quite satisfactory results can be expected.

The best containers to use are clay flower pots because these absorb moisture and prevent the plants from becoming waterlogged. Standard potting composts are suitable and seed can be sown in pots, and seedlings thinned subsequently to three or four plants to each pot. By sowing dill (*Anethum graveolens*), coriander (*Coriandrum sativum*) and chervil (*Anthriscus cerefolium*) from mid to late summer, fresh vigorous plants will be ready to take indoors in early autumn. Chives (*Allium schoenoprasm*), parsley (*Petroselinum crispum*), mint (*Mentha* species) and rooted cuttings of sage (*Salvia officinalis*) and rosemary (*Rosmarinus officinalis*) can be potted up late in the summer to establish before taking them indoors for the winter.

Light is the most important factor indoors and while a sunny window ledge may seem to be the obvious location, plants can wilt very quickly and may need to be moved away in the middle of the day. Certainly the pots will need to be turned regularly, otherwise the plants will grow one-sided and bent. Serious indoor gardeners sometimes resort to special artificial lights which provide the full spectrum of light waves for plants.

Temperature and humidity are perhaps the most tricky factors to control, especially where there is central heating to dry out the atmosphere. Pots are best set in trays of gravel which can be kept moist. Most herbs require cool night temperatures – but not the chilly conditions behind a drawn curtain on a window ledge. Where central heating is maintained at anything above 12°C

(54°F) it is advisable to remove the plants to a cooler but frost-proof utility room at night.

Spray your indoor plants occasionally to keep the leaves clean, and open a window sometimes so that they can breathe fresh air.

Conservatory plants

Aromatic and scented plants are a popular choice for a conservatory, where the atmosphere is warm and still and the structure captures the perfumes. Ideally some of the tender herbs can be enjoyed, or those that would not survive the winter out of doors in cold areas: plants such as lemon verbena (*Aloysia triphylla*) with its richly citrus-scented leaves, and all the scented-leaved geraniums (*Pelargonium* species). A range of scents is to be found here from fruit to spice, from mint to almond and if the pots are placed near a doorway where the leaves can be rubbed in passing, there is increased enjoyment to be had all year round. Some to try are *Pelargonium graveolens* (rose-scented), *P. odoratissimum* (apple-scented) and *P. tomentosum* (peppermint-scented); their pink flowers for much of the year are a bonus.

Even those herbs of Mediterranean origin which like a warm soil will need careful management in pots in a conservatory during the sunshine of summer. It is better to enjoy the decorative scented ones and pay extra attention to watering and spraying and maintain a clean environment for their cultivation.

Several herbs popular in the garden make attractive container plants suitable for the conservatory. The lavenders, especially *Lavandula stoechas* and *L.s.* ssp *pendunculata* will survive later in flower than out doors. Lily-of-the-valley (*Convallaria majalis*) can be forced in pots or baskets for early spring scent. Melilot (*Melilotus officinalis*) will provide the often absent yellow flowers for a conservatory.

Of the woody plants the Carolina allspice (*Calycanthis floridus*) with its strap-shaped petals of rusty rose, makes an attractive shrub if provided with shade and well watered. And the mainstay evergreens are myrtle (*Myrtus communis*), bay (*Laurus nobilis*), rosemary (*Rosmarinus officinalis*) and the eucalypt (*Eucalyptus citriodora*) for its lemon-scented foliage, and *E. globulus* and *E. gunnii* for their silver blue leaves which serve as a foil for other plants.

To clothe the wall of a conservatory or to wrap around a supporting post, or wander in the roof, nothing could be prettier than the white-flowered summer jasmine (*Jasminum officinale*), though its scent can be quite overpowering. The pretty leaves persist throughout the year; there is a golden-leaved form. Where space and scale permit, a large ceramic container planted with *Aloe vera* would add a dramatic statement to the herb collection. A succulent with large flat leaves edged with spines, it is none too partial to strong sunlight. It grows slowly and demands little other than an occasional drink of fluoride-free water.

A decorative collection of herbs in attractive containers can be changed often when grown in a conservatory.

·6·
Propagation

Many herbs grow from seed, some self seed readily, but the perennials need a little more understanding and are grown from division, cuttings or layers.

Seed

Some herbs are raised from seed annually, sown in the early part of the year in pots or boxes, thinned and hardened off (tempered) for about a week and planted out of doors in early summer once the soil has warmed up. Or they can be sown directly into the open ground in shallow drills during the very early summer and thinned subsequently. Seed of the Umbelliferous plants should be treated this way because they react to being disturbed and transplanted by bolting and running to seed too early. These are caraway (*Carum carvi*), dill (*Anethum graveolens*), chervil (*Anthriscus cerefolium*), and parsley (*Petroselinum crispum*).

On heavy soils, or one on which a good tilth cannot be produced easily, sprinkle a little fine soil or preparatory seed compost to enfold the seeds in the drill. Label each row with the name of the plant.

A few herbs are biennials, which means they are sown one year (usually in summer) to flower the next. Notable biennials are: clary (*Salvia sclarea*), verbascum (*Verbascum thapsus*), evening primrose (*Oenothera biennis*), melilot (*Melilotus officinalis*), mallow (*Malva sylvestris*) and fox-glove (*Digitalis purpurea*). Some biennials appear to behave as perennials, especially if the flowering stems are cut away so that the plant does not form seed.

● *Transplanting seedlings* at any stage of growth calls for extreme care. Until at least two proper leaves have formed they should not be moved. Then lift them out carefully by a leaf, without touching or disturbing the root system. Transplant into a good tilth by making a small hole first and, still holding the seedling by a leaf, drop it in and gently firm the soil around it and water in.

· HERBS TO GROW FOR SEED ·

Name	Type of plant
Angelica (*Angelica archangelica*)	Biennial
Anise (*Pimpinella anisum*)	Annual
Borage (*Borago officinalis*)	Annual
Caraway (*Carum carvi*)	Biennial
Chervil (*Anthriscus cerefolium*)	Annual
Chives (*Allium schoenoprasm*)	Perennial
Coriander (*Coriandrum sativum*)	Annual
Dill (*Anethum graveolens*)	Annual
Fennel (*Foeniculum vulgare*)	Perennial
Feverfew (*Tanacetum parthenium*)	Perennial
Hyssop (*Hyssopus officinalis*)	Perennial
Marigold (*Calendula officinalis*)	Annual
Marsh mallow (*Malva sylvestris*)	Perennial
Sorrel (*Rumex acetosa*)	Perennial
Summer savory (*Satureia hortensis*)	Annual
Sweet Cicely (*Myrrhis odorata*)	Perennial

· HANDY TIP ·

Parsley seed is notoriously slow to germinate. (It is said that it goes nine times to the Devil and back while waiting!) Soak the seeds overnight and then water the drill just before sowing with hot water from the kettle. Keep the soil watered, especially in warm weather.

Division

By dividing the roots and crowns of a plant during the dormant season, some herb stocks can be built up fairly quickly because when divided each small section already has a root. It is good gardening practice to divide some herbs, particularly invasive ones like tansy (*Tanacetum vulgare*) and mints (*Mentha* species), as well as others that waste away in the centre of the clump, like bergamot (*Monarda didyma*).

Dig up the plants, remove the old flower stem and cut back the growth close to the crown. Pull and separate or cut and tease apart pieces, each with at least one growth bud and roots. Replant firmly and keep a close watch until there are signs of regrowth, signalling fresh root activity.

Plants with wide-spreading creeping roots or stems (stolons), like soapwort (*Saponaria officinalis*), woodruff (*Asperula odorata*), mints (*Mentha* species) and mat-forming thymes such as *Thymus herba-barona*, are easy to divide. Pieces bearing roots can be disentangled from the parent plant and set out separately.

Layering

Those plants which naturally form roots on shoots that touch the ground can be layered in summer to provide new plants. Scrape or notch the stem to be layered and peg it down or hold it in place with a stone. Once roots have developed the shoot can be severed from the parent plant and planted elsewhere and watered in.

A variation is mound layering in which fine soil is piled over the centre of the plant in spring, so that only the young growth shows. Most shoots will then form roots, and by late summer there will be a number of sections that can be separated, each bearing shoots and roots.

Herbs that can be propagated by layering include: thyme (*Thymus* species, especially *T.* × *citriodorus*), sage (*Salvia officinalis*), bay (*Laurus nobilis*), lavender cotton (*Santolina* species), jasmine (*Jasminum officinalis*) and periwinkle (*Vinca major*), which tip roots readily.

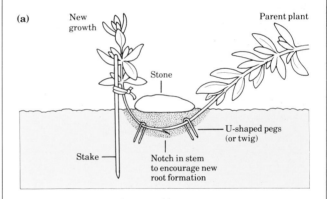

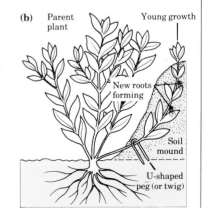

Fig. 15 A layered plant is encouraged to form new roots, then is severed from the parent.

(a) Simple layering involves taking a low branch of the plant and pegging it down.

(b) Mound layering encourages old stems to form new roots.

63

Marjoram (*Origanum* species) can be propagated from stem cuttings taken in summer.

Cuttings

Stem cuttings are the most satisfactory way in which to propagate most perennial herbs. Softwood cuttings are taken in the late spring, once there are new shoots to remove, and semi-ripe cuttings are made after midsummer, sometimes with a heel (that is, with a tiny strip of the main stem attached).

1. Taking cutting material from a plant should be done with discretion. Enough young growth must be left on the plant for it to be able to flourish and retain its shape and character.

2. Select strong pieces of growth, preferably non-flowering shoots about 5–12 cm (2–5 in) in length with a full growing tip.

3. Cut just below a leaf node – that is, the point at which a leaf is attached to the stem – making a straight and clean cut.

4. Remove the leaves very carefully from the lower third to half of the length of the cutting, taking care to avoid damaging it.

5. Dip the end into a hormone rooting powder and shake off any surplus.

6. Plant firmly (to avoid air pockets) to one third of the depth of the cuttings, either in pots or trays in a sandy compost or a proprietary seed and cutting compost. Or set them in a cold frame in the shade. Water in.

7. Cover pots and trays with a plastic bag to create a moist micro-climate that will hasten rooting. Once there is the merest sign of regrowth the bag must be removed.

8. Water and spray over, especially in warm weather, to prevent flagging.

9. Plant out in a nursery bed or in permanent positions in the autumn if the young plants are well advanced, or more probably the following spring.

10. Throughout the process keep similar-type cuttings together and remember to label each group clearly.

· PROPAGATION FROM CUTTINGS ·

Box (*Laurus nobilis*)	Sage (*Salvia officinalis*)
Curry plant (*Helichrysum serotinum*)	Southernwood (*Artemisia abrotanum*)
Hyssop (*Hyssopus officinalis*)	Tarragon (*Artemisia dracunculus*)
Lavender (*Lavandula angustifolia*)	Thyme (*Thymus* species)
Marjoram (*Origanum* species)	Wall germander (*Teucrium chamaedrys*)
Rosemary (*Rosmarinus officinalis*)	Winter savory (*Satureia montana*)
Rue (*Ruta graveolens*)	Wormwood (*Artemisia absinthium*)

· 7 ·
A–Z of Herbs

These herbs grow wild or can be cultivated in the temperate regions of northern Europe, North America and Australasia. Weather patterns and soil affect the performance of a plant and its ultimate height and character, so approximate sizes are given. Seasons are treated generally and unless stated otherwise seed should be sown in spring and roots divided in autumn or spring.

Aconite see **Monkshood**

Agrimony, church steeples
(*Agrimonia eupatoria*) Rosaceae
A common roadside plant in northern temperate regions with pretty fern-like leaves and tiny yellow flowers massed on a slender spike, the lower ones blooming first from midsummer onwards. Height 45 cm (18 in).
Part used: Leaves for a tisane. The whole plant produces a yellow dye.
Cultivation: Likes porous soils, and will tolerate full sun but grows better with shade for some part of the day.
Propagation: Seed when available from nurseries specializing in wild plants.

Angelica
(*Angelica archangelica*) Umbelliferae
A dramatic biennial that attains 2 m (6¾ ft) with stout ribbed hollow stems and large leaves spreading almost as wide. The flowers are carried in huge many-spoked mop heads of powdery yellow from summer until early autumn. Heads dry well.
Part used: Stems may be crystallized for confectionery.
Cultivation: It prefers rich damp soil and partial shade and is a splendid plant for the back of the border or as a focal point in a courtyard garden. If the number of flowering stems is restricted to one or two, the plants will usually persist for several seasons.
Propagation: Sow seed in autumn for flowering the following year. Self-sown seeds will germinate about the garden if allowed to do so.

Anise
(*Pimpinella anisum*) Umbelliferae
A tender half-hardy annual up to 45 cm (18 in) with erect stems that carry finely cut leaves on the upper part and deeply divided toothed ones below amid branching stems. The flowers are small and chalk white in summer followed by ribbed seeds, which turn brown when ripe.
Part used: Seeds as a culinary and pharmaceutical flavouring.
Cultivation: A light soil, sunshine and shelter are ideal.
Propagation: Seed, outdoors in early summer or earlier with some protection.

Harvesting and drying herbs

The correct time for harvesting each plant varies from one locality to another, or one season to the next, because it depends upon catching the plant at a critical point in its development – and that point soon passes. Most plants are richest in essential oils just prior to the flowers maturing, or if seed is the part to be collected it has to be caught ripe but before it is dispersed. It is essential to know which part of the herb is required – leaves, seed, root or whole herb; this information is given in the A–Z of Herbs.

Collect only one sort of plant material at once, putting it into shallow boxes or baskets so that it will not heat up. Never take more than can be dealt with in the time and space available because herbs wilt very soon after cutting. Preferably harvest shoots when they are dry, but not during the hottest part of the day.

Leaves and shoots are best cut from the plants rather than being pulled away. Take only a few shoots from each plant in order to leave enough growth for the plant to survive. The object of drying is to eliminate the water content as quickly as possible without loss of the essential oils. In a domestic situation herb shoots are usually dried by tying the stems loosely and suspending small bunches from the rafters of a garden shed, summerhouse or garage, even though this is a some-what hit-or-miss method. After the care given to cultivating the herbs, it is better to try to dry them in a more controlled way, which will give a quicker and more consistent result.

Spread the herbs evenly and fairly thinly over sheets of paper or on trays, keeping one herb separate from the shoots of another, and put them in a warm airy place, such as the airing cupboard with the door open. Once the material snaps easily when pressed between fingers and thumb it is dry and should be rubbed down immediately and stored. If it is allowed to lie about at this stage it will reabsorb moisture from the atmosphere.

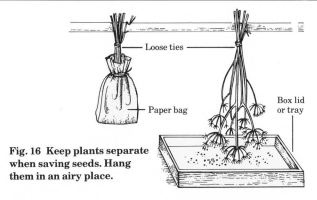

Fig. 16 Keep plants separate when saving seeds. Hang them in an airy place.

Seed destined for culinary use is taken from the whole plant which is pulled up once the seed has ripened, and the heads laid over clean paper in an airy place until the seed loosens and falls. Keep one drying head away from those of other kinds of plant. Alternatively, loose bunches of the seedheads can be tied together, and hung downwards a paper bag slipped over the heads. This method is preferable when seed is being saved for sowing (Fig. 16).

Roots are usually ripe and plump at the end of the growing season, which may be the second year for some plants, or even in the spring for plants such as Solomon's seal (*Polygonatum multiflorum*). Lift the whole root with a flat-tined potato fork to avoid bruising the skin.

Flowers are collected for inclusion in pot-pourri and scented bags just as they are coming into full flower. When petals are to be used to garnish food, take them from the plant very carefully, without bruising them.

Freezing
Most herbs can be preserved by freezing; this is useful for those that do not dry satisfactorily, such as mint (*Mentha* species), parsley (*Petroselinum crispum*) fennel (*Foeniculum vulgare*) and tarragon (*Artemisia dracunculus*). Tiny sprigs, chopped leaves or flowers can be set in ice cubes to be popped into summer drinks or used in cooking.

Balm, bergamot

(*Monarda didyma*) Labiatae

A hardy herbaceous perennial, sweetly aromatic, up to 75 cm (30 in) with oval dark green leaves and sparkler-like crimson flowers in summer. The true herb has small flowers but the cultivar 'Cambridge Scarlet' is popularly grown. The root retains the sweet aroma in winter.

Part used: Leaves infused as a tisane (Oswego tea) or floated in summer drinks. Flowers garnish salads.

Cultivation: A really fertile soil suits it best, where there is some moisture. Shade-tolerant but good light is essential for the aroma. Cut back in autumn and divide regularly as the clumps tend to become bare in the centre.

Propagation: Divide the rootstock.

Basil, sweet basil

(*Ocimum*) Labiatae

Annuals, treated as tender in all but hot climates where they are grown as perennials, with broad juicy aromatic leaves. There are two main types:

Ocimum basilicum with strongly flavoured dark pungent green leaves, 60 cm (24 in) high, and an attractive red or purple-leaved form catalogued as 'Dark Opal' with toothed leaf margins and a more spicy flavour. The flowers are somewhat insignificant, creamy white tinged purple in summer.

Bush or dwarf basil (*O*.var. *minimum*) is known also as Greek basil. It is a more compact plant, growing to 25 cm (10 in). A lemon-scented species *O. americanum* is listed.

Part used: Leaves as culinary flavouring

Cultivation: Reserve the warmest spot available for basil in full sun on light well-drained soil, and hope for a good dry summer! Bush basil grows well as a pot plant or crowns can be cut back, lifted and potted up late in the summer. Will survive indoors well into the autumn to provide fresh leaves.

Propagation: Seed sown under glass or with protection in early spring; plant out 15 cm (6 in) apart when likelihood of frost has passed. Make a summer sowing in pots, planting out later, to ensure a supply of fresh leaves.

Bay, sweet bay

(*Laurus nobilis*) Lauracea

A semi-evergreen often restricted by clipping but in favourable localities develops into a tree 12 m (40 ft) high. Normally seen as a large shrub up to 2 m (6¾ ft), or as a hedge. It has smooth dark green oval leaves which are pungent and leathery, and small creamy white flowers amid the foliage in clusters in early summer, sometimes followed by dark purple berries. Male and female flowers are carried on separate plants.

Part used: Leaves used as culinary flavouring for their pungent oil. Classical hereos were crowned with wreaths of bay; and terms 'Poet Laureat' and the French 'baccalaureat' derive from this.

Cultivation: Bay needs shelter from cold winds, which will 'burn' the foliage, and also protection from frosts in severe winters or during prolonged periods of very low temperatures. It likes a well-drained soil with other plants around it. It is commonly cultivated as a container plant for balconies, doorways and foyers, when it is clipped to shape.

Propagation: Layering of the lower branches. Very difficult from cuttings taken in autumn.

Bergamot see Balm

Betony, wood betony

(*Stachys officinalis*) Labiatae

A perennial herb 30–45 cm (12–18 in) with oval green leaves regularly veined and toothed

varying considerably in size. They have strong astringent properties. Rose-purple flowers are carried in a firm spike above the foliage in summer. Earlier flowers appear between the leaves. There is a white-flowered form *S.o. alba*, but for the decorative herb garden a clump of the larger growing cultivar *S.o.* 'Rosea Superba', with its richer flowers is invaluable.

Part used: Dried leaves as an infusion as a calming tonic or an ingredient of snuff. (Do not use leaves fresh.)

Cultivation: It prefers semi-shade and a fertile soil. Cut back to the old rosette of leaves in the autumn and divide and replant every third year to keep the clumps bold.

Propagation: Seed or division for the type. 'Rosea Superba' is divided, or daughter plants pulled away and planted out separately.

Borage

(*Borago officinalis*) Boraginaceae

A sturdy annual that can reach 90 cm (36 in) but is usually less, with stout bristly stems and rough leaves. The flower heads are silvered by hairs that give the appearance of spun glass and bestow a frostiness to the plant. Flowers deep azure blue, starry, sometimes white.

Part used: Leaves can be used for their cucumber flavour and flowers for garnishing salads and summer drinks.

Cultivation: Best on poor dry soils, even shallow ones, and therefore never as successful when grown in a container. Give it full sun. It will self seed.

Propagation: Seed sown in situ autumn or mid-summer, but only the tiniest seedlings will transplant. Some experimenting may be needed.

◀ **Hoary flower heads of borage (*Borago officinalis*) add a sparkle throughout the summer.**

Burdock, gypsy's rhubarb, beggar's buttons

(*Arctum lappa*) Compositae
A truly handsome plant, upstanding and reaching 2 m (6¾ ft) in height with enormous triangular leaves which spread out in layers around the central and lateral stems. The flowers are deep red in late summer and develop into the hooked burs beloved of children.
Part used: Young stalks can be eaten as a vegetable, as in Japan, or can be candied. Leaves are believed to have antibiotic properties; also used in the making of a domestic beer. Root as an infusion to clear the blood.
Cultivation: Requires a moist soil and will tolerate fairly deep shade.
Propagation: Sow fresh seed in autumn in either sun or shade for growing the following year.

Caraway

(*Carum carvi*) Umbelliferae
A biennial growing to about 60 cm (24 in) and spreading as much in maturity. Soft feathery green aromatic foliage. Tiny white flowers carried in small flat umbels bloom in the second half of summer.
Part used: Seeds for flavouring, fresh leaf sprigs for flavouring salads.
Cultivation: It will grow in any well-drained soil in a sunny position and is a good if unpretentious mid-border plant. Pick the flower heads before seeds ripen, otherwise seed will explode and be lost. As with all umbelliferous plants, the seed will continue to ripen on the heads after gathering.
Propagation: Sow seed spring or autumn and subsequently thin but do not transplant.

Chamomile, Roman chamomile

(*Chamaemelum nobile*) Compositae
A hardy evergreen small plant, usually not more than 20–25 cm (8–10 in) and often sprawling up to 15 cm (6 in) and therefore low growing. Foliage is soft, grassy and feathery, and richly aromatic of apples with daisy/chalk-white flowers all summer; a double-flowered form is *C.n.* 'Flore Pleno'. Use the non-flowering 'Treneague' for lawns.
Part used: Flower heads for cosmetic and medicinal use.
Cultivation: On a well-drained soil a group of plants put in about 10 cm (4 in) apart each way will soon make a pretty patch around the base of a sundial or bird bath, or can be grown to form a bench or pathway. Clip occasionally to keep within bounds.
Propagation: Division of the rootstock in early spring or summer cuttings or seed. Keep the soil moist around tiny plants until established.

Chervil

(*Anthriscus cerefolium*) Umbelliferae
An annual, at its best when young, that reaches 40 cm (16 in) with fern-like dark green leaves and typical umbelliferous white flowers in summer.
Part used: Fresh leaves used in cooking for their pungent flavour.
Cultivation: A mid-border plant that prefers shade and light well-drained soil with some added compost or other moisture-retentive material.
Propagation: Seed, sown at three-week intervals to maintain a succession. Do not transplant.

Chicory

(*Cichorium intybus*) Compositae
A perennial reaching 90 cm–1.5 m (3–5 ft), but spreading only about 60 cm (24 in) with jagged leaves reminiscent of the dandelion (*Taraxacum officinale*). Exquisite clear blue flowers are studded along the stem-like stars and fade from midday; more flower the following morning. There is a pink-flowered form.
Part used: Roots for medicine, leaves for salads.

Cultivation: Best on a none-too-dry alkaline soil, where smaller plants can shade its base to keep it cool, although it needs to have its head in the sun. A back-of-the-border plant especially for informal planting. Young leaves of the spring rosette can be blanched to use in salads by covering with an upturned pot or seakale-forcing pot. Or crowns earthed up well (as for potatoes) in autumn will provide early tender shoots in most winters.

Propagation: Division of rootstock in spring or autumn, or from seed when obtainable.

Chives

(*Allium schoenoprasm*) Liliaceae

A clump-forming perennial with hollow grass-like leaves that stand up well and enhance the mauve bobble-like flowers in late spring and early summer. Up to 45 cm (18 in) but often smaller. There is a white-flowered form, not often seen, with papery flowers and 'Forescate' with rich rose pink flowers.

Part used: Fresh leaves as a flavouring.

Cultivation: Prefers sandy loam, tolerant of chalk but does not thrive easily on heavy moist soils. Dappled shade or afternoon shade suits them.

Propagation: Root division or sow seed as early as possible when the soil warms up or under glass in late winter, in pots, thinning later then planting out where required.

Comfrey, boneset

(*Symphytum officinale*) Boraginaceae

A stout perennial 60–90 cm (24–36 in) with broad hairy lanceolete basil leaves, and some held singly up the rough stem. One-sided clusters of tubular bell-shaped flowers curl back at the top of each stem, usually pink and white or cream but sometimes blue, and variants are common. *S. ×uplandicum* is cultivated as a fodder crop and for composting.

Part used: Root and leaves as compress, forerunner of plaster-of-Paris. Do not apply directly to the skin.

Cultivation: Comfrey revels in deep damp soils and watery situations such as the banks of a pond or stream. Both shade and sun suit it. Left undisturbed it will spread rapidly. Remove flowering stems if it is grown for composting to encourage leaf production.

Propagation: Division or root cuttings either in spring or autumn, pieces of chopped-up root will often grow.

Coriander

(*Coriandrum sativum*) Umbelliferae

A hardy annual of dainty appearance up to 60 cm (24 in) high with lower leaves fan-like and the upper ones a filigree of green. Tiny mauve-pink flowers in umbels appear in midsummer and ripen into buff-ridged seeds. The plant emits an unpleasant odour just before the seeds ripen.

Part used: Fresh foliage and seed for flavouring in cooking.

Cultivation: Most fertile soils, and the plants may need some twiggy support. Choose a sunny sheltered spot.

Propagation: Seed sown thinly; notably slow to germinate.

Costmary see Tansy

Dill

(*Anethum graveolens*) Umbelliferae

A hardy annual 1.2–1.5 m (4–5 ft) high with delicate thread-like foliage, pale green, and umbels of yellow flowers in summer. Round aromatic seeds look striking in early autumn.

Part used: Fresh leaves to flavour fish, potatoes and pickles. The pungent seed to flavour vinegar. Anti-flatulence medicine.

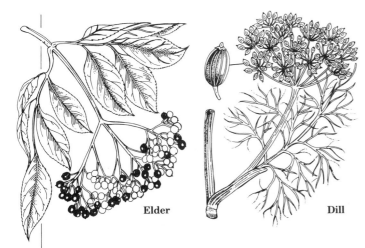

Elder   Dill

Cultivation: Dill thrives on a good light soil with full sunlight.

Propagation: Sow seed in shallow drills and thin out later. Do not transplant.

Elder

(*Sambucus nigra*) Caprifoliaceae

A quick-growing deciduous shrub or small tree 9 m (30 ft) high, with strong-smelling, oval toothed green leaves and broad flat heads of tiny white sweet-smelling flowers in midsummer. Luscious wine red or black berries follow in autumn, at which time the leaves often assume a rosy flush. Long associated with protective magic, hence there are superstitions about cutting it down. Do not eat uncooked berries, as the purgative action is fierce.

Part used: Berries in preserves, syrups and wines. Leaves used externally as eye wash.

Cultivation: It prefers heavy soils and full sunshine but is fairly easily pleased elsewhere. It provides a windbreak where there is space, although its winter appearance is not good. Can be cut back quite severely in autumn and will regenerate easily.

Propagation: Hardwood cuttings with a heel strike quickly if taken at midsummer, just before the flowers bloom.

Elecampane, scabwort

(*Inula helenium*) Compositae

A handsome perennial growing up to 90 cm (36 in) with large oval leaves, hairy below, which are stemless and diminish in size as they reach the flower heads. The flowers are wide daisy-like, bright yellow with thin strap-like petals, sometimes like a fringe, and form clusters. They open in succession from midsummer. A good back-of-the-border plant in the informal herb garden where late summer foliage is hidden.

Part used: Young shoots for candying; leaves as animal ointment.

Cultivation: Tolerant of most soils including chalk, if prepared and where there is sunshine. Replace about every third year.

Propagation: Division of rootstock, preferably in spring.

Evening primrose, moonflower

(*Oenothera biennis*) Onagraceae

A biennial which forms a rosette of leaves during the first year and a reddish rough flowering stem up to 1 m (3¼ ft) high the following season. The leaves are broadly tongue-shaped bright green with a red mid-rib, and are carried right up the stem. The flowers are flimsy and poppy-like, pale yellow and rather conspicuous all summer and into the autumn. They scent the evening garden. All parts of the plant are edible; the roots are parsnip-like.

Part used: Seed for the production of oil, and roots which in recent years have gained considerable credibility and enthusiasm from orthodox medicine in both the U.K. and N. America and Canada. The plant lives up to its ancient name of King's cure-all.

Cultivation: Tolerant, but shows a preference for a light well-drained soil in full sun.

Propagation: Seed. It self seeds freely.

The one-sided cluster of tubular flowers of comfrey (*Symphytum officinale*) are carried on a rough stem.

► A small bed of herbs as part of a larger garden with bronze fennel, sage and lavender.

Fennel

(*Foeniculum vulgare*) Umbelliferae
A hardy perennial growing up to 50 cm–1.2 m (2½–4 ft) with thick hollow stems and abundant filmy feathery deep green foliage aromatic of anise, and in the form *F.v.*var. *purpureum* bronze brown-black. Tiny yellow flowers in flat umbels in midsummer. A highly decorative plant.
Part used: Foliage for culinary flavouring.
Cultivation: Shelter from stiff breezes on a fertile soil that is mulched with compost each autumn. Grow as a group rather than individually for best effect.
Propagation: Division or seed, but allow enough space when planting out. Alternatively, offsets can be detached from the base of the plants and set out separately in spring.

Fenugreek see **Greek hayseed**
Feverfew see **Tansy**

Foxglove, fairy thimbles

(*Digitalis purpurea*) Scrophulariaceae
A biennial with fibrous root which produces a rosette of soft oval leaves the first year then reaches 1–1.5m (3–5 ft) before flowering the second summer. Thimble like, spotted purple flower bells hang down one side of the stem. Many ornamental forms, and *D. lutea* with glossy leaves and yellow flowers has a place in the herb garden.
Part used: Leaves provide the drug digitalin.
Cultivation: A fertile well-drained soil, tolerant of shade.
Propagation: Seed; it will self seed. In severe winters protect seedlings with hand cloche.

Greek hayseed, fenugreek

(*Trigonella foenum-graecum*) Leguminosae
A half-hardy annual in cooler temperate regions, growing up to 60 cm (24 in) high with creamy yellow flowers in midsummer. The leaves are typical trifoliate, soft green with a sheen. In warmer regions trigonella reaches maturity very quickly and produces typical pods containing square aromatic seed particularly rich in vitamins. Known best as a spicy ingredient of curry powder, or as a coffee substitute with a somewhat pungent flavour.
Part used: Seed as flavouring. When soaked makes a maple syrup flavour which enhances confectionery. Can also be used as a cattle-fodder sweetener.
Cultivation: Fairly unselective of soil but requiring moisture for both germination and growth.
Propagation: Seed sown any time under suitable conditions. Sow small amounts regularly through spring and summer to ensure a succession of tasty leaves.

Ground ivy, alehoof

(*Glechoma hederacea*) Labiatae

A hardy perennial, strong smelling, and lax in habit, up to 10 cm (4 in) and spreading 30 cm (12 in) and providing rapid ground cover. The leaves are downy, dark green and heart-shaped, and marbled with silver. They bear glands that contain the aromatic and bitter oil. Flowers are deep throated and bluish in early summer, and continue until autumn.

Part used: Leaves infused as a popular folk remedy for a variety of ailments, and to clarify and flavour ale before the introduction of hops.

Cultivation: A plant that almost cultivates itself. It prefers a well-drained soil in some shade, and therefore relishes a hedge-base position. Pull growth away or cut back to restrain it.

Propagation: Almost automatic if a piece is pulled away from the parent plant and planted out.

Hop

(*Humulus lupulus*) Cannabidaceae

A perennial climber, twining clockwise to 6 m (20 ft) with rough deeply lobed pale green leaves on long stalks. Better for garden use is the golden-leaved form (*H.l.* 'Aureus'). Male and female flowers are carried on separate plants: the male forms loose clusters, the female rounded heads which develop into the familiar papery cones of many overlapping bracts, among which the bitter oil lupulin is to be found.

Part used: Dried herbs to preserve liquor longer than other natural additives. To stuff pillows to act as a tranquillizer. Young shoots may be eaten as vegetables.

Cultivation: Well prepared soil, deeply worked with the addition of compost or other organic material in an open sunny position. Ideally prepare the site in the autumn ready for early spring planting. Invaluable as a climber for posts and arches in the herb garden. Grow the female form. Cut right back to ground level in the autumn.

Propagation: Cuttings in summer or from suckers cut away and planted out in summer and kept watered. They will bear the third year after planting.

Houseleek, thunder plant

(*Sempervivum tectorum*) Crassulaceae

A hardy tough perennial rising only to 5 cm (2 in) above the ground but spreading in a conglomerate rosette to 12 cm (5 in) on maturity. The leaves are wedge shaped, thick and always cool to the touch, smooth green, often suffused with pink or rusty rose. Each leaf is a living reservoir, enabling the plant to survive in barren conditions. Habitually grown on roofs, and in folk-lore believed to ward off evil spirits and prevent lightning from striking.

Part used: Leaves bruised or crushed to relieve inflammation. Also used to clear grit from eyes.

Cultivation: The barest stonework or wall or in crannies are the places the houseleek likes to grow. Once established, colonies of rosetttes will form and be trouble-free plants.

Propagation: Plant the tiny offsets at any time of the year wherever there is a porous root run. Very slow to establish.

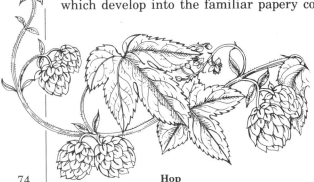

Hop

Hyssop

Lavender

Hyssop

(*Hyssopus officinalis*) Labiatae

A semi-evergreen hardy perennial reaching 60 cm (24 in) and forming a bushy burst of stems all from the base of the plant, with small, spicy, dark green leaves. Tiny flowers are borne all summer, generally blue, but there are pink and white forms.

Part used: Flowers and shoots for flavouring house-hold remedies for a whole range of ailments. It contains an antiseptic oil, which is an ingredient of eau de Cologne. May be added to pot-pourri.

Cultivation: Select a sunny spot on a fairly dry soil for the best results (situation can affect the refinement of the aroma). Cut back in autumn or early spring. Replace every fourth year.

Propagation: Division or seed, or summer cuttings.

Lavender

(*Lavandula angustifolia*) Labiatae

A perennial evergreen bush or sub-shrub growing to 30–75 cm (1–2½ ft) in height and spreading as far, and thriving in all but the cold mid-continental winters of east Europe and central N. America. The long narrow leaves are downy and aromatic, especially when young, and vary from grey to green in some of the cultivars. The flower heads are carried on stiff, grey, upstanding stalks that exceed the rounded cushion-like growth of the leaves to give an appearance in midsummer of a pincushion spiked with hatpins. The flowers are a gentle blue-mauve held in rolled heads. The woody base stem becomes gnarled and twisted with age (described as leggy) when the bush tends to lean heavily to one side.

The species is sometimes classified as *Lavandula officinalis*, and *L. vera* and *L. spica*, especially in the past but these names are now believed to refer to *L × intermedia*, often called Dutch lavender. Varieties to grow include 'Hidcote', a free and brilliant blue-flowered smaller plant; 'Munstead', lavender blue with narrow green leaves; and 'Grosso', larger, up to 45 cm (18 in) with big flower heads of deep purplish blue. All are invaluable for bordering paths or block planting. The French lavender *L. stoechas* is considerably less hardy and only about 30 cm (12 in) high with fly away petals as a top knot to the purple-rose flowers on stalks which do not rise much above the foliage. The form *L.s.ssp. pedunculata* is a striking novelty: each flower head carries two large petals on top which look like exotic butterflies hovering above the plant.

Part used: Leaves and flowers as an insect repellent, or to add to pot-pourri, or to flavour desserts. Oil of lavender is prized as an antiseptic healer and cosmetic ingredient.

Cultivation: A lover of poor soils including chalk, but it needs full sunshine. Cut back quite hard regularly and be prepared to replace plants when they become gawky.

Propagation: Cuttings at any time; summer is best.

Lavender cotton, cotton lavender
(*Santolina* species) Compositae

Santolina chamaecyparissus with thread-like foliage reminiscent of coral, forms a cushion of strongly camphorous growth. The small yellow bobble flowers decorate the plant in high summer. *S. neapolitana* is slightly taller up to 60 cm (24 in) and softer in growth with greener leaves and paler flowers; catalogued as 'Sulphurea'. *S. virens* (also known as *S. rosmarinifolia rosmarinifolia*) has compact growth 30 cm (12 in) with emerald green foliage and is richly aromatic and oily to handle. Yellow flowers in summer. All make first-rate edging plants.

Stout hollow stems and shining, much-divided leaves are characteristic features of the handsome lovage.

Part used: Shoots dried as insecticide.

Cultivation: A light well-drained soil in good light is ideal. Where they are grown at a lawn edge it is advisable to place a paving stone in front of each plant to prevent them from rotting from below on the damp turf. Clip closely in spring to encourage new well-coloured growth and to prevent legginess and bare patches.

Propagation: Summer cuttings or layering in late summer or early autumn.

Lemon balm, bee balm
(*Melissa officinalis*) Labiatae

A hardy perennial forming a dense clump up to 90 cm (36 in) with rather proud ovate, wrinkled, bright green leaves strongly aromatic of lemon when crushed. The creamy white flowers in midsummer are insignificant and rather fleeting. Valued by beekeepers.

Part used: Young leaves as an infusion or culinary flavouring.

Cultivation: Tolerant of poor soil provided not too dry, in a good sunny spot. Tends to spread.

Propagation: Division, seed or stem cuttings in late spring.

Lovage
(*Levisticum officinale*) Umbelliferae

A hardy perennial, slow to develop but reaching 90 cm–1 m (3–3¼ ft) with substantial hollow stems and large much-divided leaves, shining green above the paler below. Yellow flowers, carried in umbels in summer are followed by curved seeds.

Part used: Leaves and young shoots as culinary flavouring.

Cultivation: Prefers slightly acid well-prepared soil and dappled shade or full sun. Not successful in a container. A good back-of-the-border plant.

Propagation: Division of rootstock or seed.

Lungwort, Jerusalem cowslip

(*Pulmonaria officinalis*) Boraginaceae
A herbaceous perennial up to 20 cm (8 in) high, and spreading as much to make good ground cover quite quickly. Flat, pointed, green, rough leaves splashed with white and small clusters of bell flowers that change from pink to blue. The spotted leaves were considered to suggest diseased lungs in the *Doctrine of Signatures*, a cult very fashionable in the seventeenth century where each plant was believed to offer a clue to its intended use.

Part used: Leaves which can be chopped for salads. An infusion, long used to relieve pulmonary complaints.

Cultivation: A good plant for shade and a moist soil.

Propagation: Division or seed.

Marigold

(*Calendula officinalis*) Compositae
A hardy annual that sometimes persists through more than one season, up to 45 cm (18 in). Leaves lanceolate bright green and stalkless. Orange daisy-like flowers are in bloom for much of the year as the name *Calendula* suggests. The true herb has small flowers with one row of petals but there are numerous double-flowered forms offered by seedsmen.

Part used: Petals, dried or fresh for flavouring and colouring food. Traditionally a cosmetic herb and used for the treatment of skin disorders.

Cultivation: Successful on most soils except heavy or damp ones, but prefers a sunny spot. Remove old flower heads regularly to ensure continued flowering.

Propagation: Seed can be sown in autumn but spring seed is more successful and seedlings need to be at least 30 cm (12 in) apart to allow for development. Marigolds self seed readily.

Containers are used effectively to soften the change in path textures and the edge of the border.

Marjoram, oregano

(*Origanum species*) Labiatae
There are several slightly tender species of *Origanum*. The principal ones for the herb border are: sweet or knotted marjoram (*Origanum majorana*), wild marjoram (*O. vulgare*) and pot marjoram (*O. onites*).

Sweet marjoram (*O. majorana*) is a perennial, usually cultivated as an annual, growing up to 45 cm (18 in). The leaves are soft, small and green, and pleasantly fragrant. The pale mauve and white flowers are tiny and 'knotted' together in summer and the stem has often a reddish tinge.

Pot marjoram (*O. onites*), also known as French marjoram, is taller at 60 cm (24 in) and forms a stronger plant with bushy habit, spreading 25–45 cm (10–18 in). The leaves are broadly heart shaped, bright green, less sweet in flavour with white or pink flowers in summer.

Wild marjoram (*O. vulgare*) is often called oregano. (In some countries, notably Mexico and the southern United States, oregano is a colloquial name for unrelated plants which have similar pungent flavours.) A stouter plant, leggy, up to 60–75 cm (24–30 in). The leaves are often tiny and strongly pungent, sometimes turning back down the stem, and the flowers are carried in a more colourful head, rosy purple with longer throats than other species. For decorative-leaved marjorams see page 39.

Part used: Leaves and flower tips for culinary flavouring and garnishing. Ingredient of pot-pourri.

Cultivation: All marjorams grow best in well-drained light soil in a warm position in the sunniest corner. Keep young plants coming along each season for the best supply in terms of flavour and appearance.

Propagation: Sow seed for sweet marjoram in the spring, with protection. For others, but plants initially and take summer cuttings to maintain a stock, then the rootstocks can be divided in subsequent seasons.

Marsh mallow
(*Althea officinalis*) Malvaceae
A tall hardy perennial at least 1 m (3¼ ft) high with broad lobed downy leaves. Flowers rather small, pale pink in late summer.

Part used: Seed heads eaten fresh or foliage dried and infused to make an eye bath. Infused roots act as a digestive.

Cultivation: A good plant for maritime areas; will tolerate brackish soil and salt winds. Otherwise select a moisture-retentive soil. Good for the back of the border.

Propagation: Divide the long roots or sow seed to produce stout rich spires of flowers the following year.

Mignonette
(*Reseda odorata*) Resedaceae
A hardy annual forming a rosette of round strap-like leaves and a flower stem up to 45 cm (18 in) high, bearing spires of tiny green-white flowers with conspicuous orange stamens in summer. The entire plant emits a delicious almond scent. Wild mignonette (*R. lutea*) is a similar, scentless plant. Weld (*R. lutea*) is a good dye plant and upright mignonette (*R. alba*) is a short-lived perennial and more strongly scented than other species.

Part used: Whole plant for the commercial production of oil used in perfumery. Add flowers and leaves to pot-pourri.

Cultivation: Thrives best in a sunny border where the soil is a bit limy or loosened with old rubble. Water during hot weather. With *Reseda odorata* pinch out the main flowering shoot as it forms as a way of encouraging bushy plants and scented flowers.

Propagation: Sow seed broadcast or in drills in spring and later thin to 10 cm (4 in) apart. The seed remains fertile for some years and may well spring up where soil has been newly disturbed.

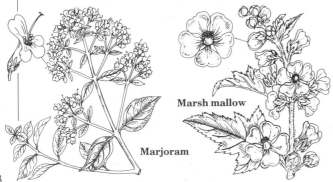

Marsh mallow

Marjoram

> **· HANDY TIP ·**
>
> All the mints (*Mentha* species) are quick growing and very invasive. Rope-like stems run just below the surface of the soil. To retain them sink a large bottomless container into the border and plant into that. Or bury bricks or tiles on end to contain the roots.

Mint

(*Mentha* species) Labiatae

Hardy herbaceous perennials that spread rapidly by stoloniferous stems along the surface of the soil. Leaves are carried in opposite pairs alternating along square stems and are highly aromatic when rubbed or broken. Generally the flowers are carried in spikes above the foliage.

Apple mint, Egyptian mint (*M. suaveolens*) has rounded downy leaves and a clear crisp apple flavour. 90 cm (3 ft). The flowers are a dusky pink. A smaller growing form, popularly recognized as apple mint, is *M.s.* 'Variegata' marked with cream and white. It is a familiar plant for border edges. It does not flower as freely as the other types, but when it does the heads are terminal, purplish mauve on spikes which tend to curve. It persists further into the winter months than any other mint.

Bergamot mint or eau de Cologne mint (*M. × p. citrata*) has far rounder leaves than piperita forms. A rich reddish purple is suffused over the leaf, especially around the leaf margins.

Bowles mint (*M. × villosa* 'Alopercuroides') grows to 1 m (3¼ ft), with broad richly hairy leaves that are soft to the touch and with a strong aroma.

Garden mint, spearmint (*M. spicata*) is the commonly cultivated plant with the mint sauce aroma, 60 cm (24 in) high. The leaves are bright clear green; its former name was *M. viridis*,

meaning 'green', which distinguishes it from all other mints. The flowers come in the late summer and are purplish mauve, carried in a series of little whorls around the stem, sometimes as many as a dozen.

Ginger mint or spicy mint (*M. × gentilis*), 45 cm (18 in) high, has smooth green leaves strongly splashed with yellow or coral red in the form *M. × g.* 'Variegata' and with a very spicy aroma.

Lemon mint (*Mentha aquatica citrata*) (15–90 cm (6–36 in) with rounded leaves, shining dark green and suffused purple when well grown in damp conditions. Strongly aromatic of fresh lemon-mint with an acrid flavour. The flowers vary from mauve to a rose pink and are borne in rounded heads.

Pennyroyal or pudding grass (*M. pulegium*) is a ground hugging plant with dark shining leaves. The flower stems stand up to about 10 cm (4 in) in late summer with a series of ball-like pink flower heads strung along the stem, the smallest at the top and then finished off with a pair of tiny leaves. A form has been developed and is catalogued as upright pennyroyal in which the flower stems are taller and more erect. Grows to 30 cm (12 in).

Peppermint (*M. × piperita*), growing to 45 cm (18 in), is the plant from which peppermint oil is obtained. The form with deep metallic bronze purple stems is black peppermint. The leaves are relatively long and narrow and the flowers in summer are purple in a terminal spike. (This plant is a natural hybrid between *M. aquatica* and *M. spicata*).

All mints hybridize easily and vary in aroma and stature according to the growing conditions, season and locality. These disparities have led to a range of vernacular tags, and inconsistencies in herb catalogues. The beginner must not be discouraged: once you have got used to and can recognize a few standard species such as are suggested here their names will become familiar and you can enjoy cultivating mints to the full.

Part used: Leaves as culinary, medicinal, pharmaceutical and confectionery flavouring. An infusion of the better flavoured ones makes a pleasant tisane.

Cultivation: All mints prefer a moist rich soil in half shade, although the mint bed must not be allowed to become dank, otherwise flavours are inferior. Beds need to be cleared every third year. (It is a traditional practice to burn off the plants each autumn, top dress with compost and replant. This disposes of old stringy runners and eliminates weeds.)

Propagation: There is almost no need to propagate mints, the runners pulled away from the parent plant usually have roots attached and when replanted will spread quickly.

Apple mint (*Mentha suaveolens* 'Variegata') makes a good edging plant and persists well into the winter.

Monkshood, helmet flower, aconite

(*Aconitum napellus*) Ranunculacae
A hardy perennial with tuberous root up to 90 cm (36 in) with dark deeply lobed leaves all along the stem. Flowers are royal blue, helmet-like, carried in a spike in summer.

Part used: Whole plant, leaves and tops fresh; and the root dried to produce the drug aconite.

Highly poisonous. The cultivars 'Bicolor' (blue and white flowers), 'Ivorine' (early flowering with cream flowers) and 'Bressingham Spire' (deep violet blue flowers and foliage held well around the plant), are all impressive in the herb border.

Cultivation: Likes semi-shaded, moist position. Cut back in autumn as it dies down in winter.

Propagation: Root division.

Mullein, Aaron's rod

(*Verbascum thapsus*) Scrophulariaceae
A true biennial reaching 2m (6¾ ft) in height the second year. A distinctive basal rosette is formed in the first year of large silver leaves 30 cm (12 in) long, felt-like to touch and in appearance. The proud flower spike clothed along the stem with smaller leaves which diminish in size and number carries bright yellow flowers at midsummer. A good back-of-the-border plant where it can be given sufficient space for the rosette to receive enough light during the first summer to develop. It has earned the name of hag's taper from the former practice of dipping the hairy stiff stem in tallow or suet to use as a torch or rush light.

Part used: Leaves for the relief of pulmonary disorders as an ingredient of herbal tobacco.

Cultivation: It grows in any well-drained soil. When it is too damp the woolly leaves tend to rot and need to be removed. It can be grown in a grassy situation provided there is sunshine.

Propagation: Seed sown in autumn or spring. It will self sow about the garden.

Opium poppy

(*Papaver somniferum*) Papaveraceae

An annual up to 1m (3¼ ft) high with large jagged-edged leaves that clasp the stem and are rather glaucous, paler below. The hairy stems support solitary flowers with silky thin pink, mauve or dull red petals, sometimes single but more usually double in garden forms. The censer-like seed head contains numerous seeds which are not narcotic and may be used to flavour bread.

Part used: Seed heads in the production of

Pink and red large pompon flowers of the opium poppy (*Papaver somniferum*) with *Santolina rosemarinifolia*.

morphine. While this plant has led to untold human misery, it has also provided among the most valuable painkillers known to medicine.

Cultivation: Tolerant of any soil including chalk, provided that it is not sticky and cold.

Propagation: Seed. They self sow readily.

Oregano see **Marjoram**

Parsley

(*Petroselinum crispum*) Umbelliferae

A biennial that develops a thick clump of leaves during the first season and a flower stem up to 60 cm (24 in) the next, or earlier when the plants bolt. The familiar curled, crumpled leaves are rich green and fragrant, the flowers uninteresting tiny yellowish-green in umbels, that signal the end of a good flavour for the leaves. The plain-leaved (uncurled) parsley (*P. hortense*) has flat deeply indented leaves and a stronger flavour. The Hamburg parsley (*P. sativus tuberosum*) produces in the second year a tap root resembling a carrot which can be used as a vegetable.

Part used: Leaves for flavouring and garnishing.

Cultivation: All parsleys need a fertile moist soil with a good tilth and an ample supply of water to develop lush foliage. Prevent the plants from flowering to maintain good green leaves. Plants die back during severe winters.

Propagation: Seed. Try sowing in soil blocks to make transplanting easier. There are numerous theories concerning the notoriously slow germination of parsley seed. Water the drills before sowing, soak the seed overnight beforehand and cover after sowing with dry soil to act as a mulch. Keep well watered during dry weather until germination. Thin seedlings carefully to about 25 cm (10 in) apart.

Periwinkle

(*Vinca major*) Apocynaceae

A hardy evergreen perennial with long arching growths up to 1.2m (4 ft) but because of the lax habit rising only to 60–75 cm (24–30 in). Leaves are oval, pointed, glossy green, and the flowers an attractive azure blue with 'spinning' petals. The whole plant has a binding wrapping growth. There are several garden forms: *Vinca major*, a smaller plant with blue flowers; and *V.m. alba* with white flowers. Plum-purple ones are in *V.m.* 'Atropurpurea' and *V.m.* 'Burgundy'.

Part used: Leaves and roots in herbal medicine.

Cultivation: Unselective of soil provided there is some shade. It can be cut back in autumn or spring to retain growth and provide fresh shoots.

Propagation: Periwinkle layers itself wherever the arching branches touch the ground. Sever in autumn and plant out separately.

Rosemary

(*Rosmarinus officinalis*) Labiatae

An evergreen shrub 1.5–2 m (5–6¾ ft) high in sheltered situations, with decorative spiky dark green foliage which is richly resinous. Powder blue flowers nestle among the leaves from early spring to early summer, sometimes beginning in the winter months. There is a white-flowered form *R.o.var. albiflorus*. Good cultivars to grow are 'Miss Jessopp's Upright' a strong-growing somewhat fastigiate form; and 'Severn Sea', a smaller shrub with brilliant blue flowers on arching branches.

R. lavandulaceus forms a low-growing mass, studded with blue flowers in spring and is useful

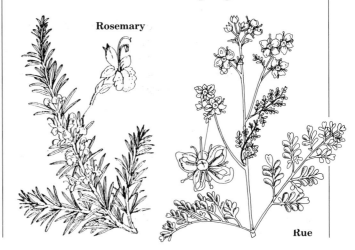

Rosemary

Rue

for draping on banks or along low walls or at the side of steps.

Part used: Foliage for the oil used in hair cosmetics, and for culinary flavouring. Add to pot-pourri with restraint.

Cultivation: Most soils are suitable including chalk, where there is good drainage and sun-shine. In colder localities wall protection will be advantageous and in mid-continental climates, some protection is needed during the winter. Rosemary is a good hedge plant and may be cultivated in a large container.

Propagation: Cuttings in summer, or layering the lower branches in summer and severing the following spring.

Rue, herb of grace

(*Ruta graveolens*) Rutaceae
A semi-evergreen perennial with woody stem 60–75 cm (24–30 in) and forming a bush that spreads about 60 cm (24 in). Leaves well divided into blue-green leaflets, flowers small and yellow with separate petals and upstanding stamens. The whole plant has a strongly distinctive odour, unpleasant to some people. Grown for its decora-tive usefulness but formerly in the treatment of insanity and epilepsy. One of the old strewing herbs used for keeping vermin and insects at bay. There are three leaf forms; the green (above), a blue-green leaved form 'Jackman's Blue' and a variegated one *R.g.* 'Variegata'.

Part used: Leaves, rarely, as insect repellent and for medicinal use.

Cultivation: Well-drained fertile soil where there is dappled shade around mid-day. Cut back to shape if necessary after flowering in alternate years.

Propagation: Late summer cuttings, essential for the superior coloured-leaved forms to ensure the true plant.

· HANDY TIP ·

If the aroma and flavour of sage (*Salvia officinalis*) appear musty and dry, either move the bush or plant rooted cuttings or layers in another part of the garden. When sage is happy it will give a fresh pungent scent. Such improvement in aroma is more pronounced for sage than for most herbs.

Sage

(*Salvia officinalis*) Labiatae
A shrubby semi-evergreen, likely to lose many leaves in really cold regions, 90–105 cm (3–3½ ft), of rather floppy habit, with tough, much-pitted and wrinkled oval grey-green leaves of dry pun-gent aroma and flavour. Long-throated lavender flowers in summer. There is a white-flowered form *S.o.* 'Alba'. The coloured-leaved kinds are not the ones to grow for culinary use but they have an important role in the decorative herb garden. They are *S.o.* 'Purpurascens' with suede-like leaves of plum purple and *S.o.* 'Tricolor' with pink, cream and green blotches together on the leaves, and known as painted lady.

The pineapple sage (*S. rutilans*) is a totally different plant, tender up to 45 cm (18 in) with soft dark green leaves sometimes suffused dark red and richly scented of pineapple. Red flowers in summer. It can be used like summer bedding in warm temperate zone areas. A useful conserva-tory herb when container grown.

Part used: Leaves as a culinary flavouring.

Cultivation: A rich dry soil in a sunny position protected from stiff breezes is best for garden sage. Cut back every alternate year after flower-ing and if the flavour is not good, move the plant, or put out rooted cuttings in another part of the garden. More than any other plant, sage needs to

▲ A variegated sage (*Salvia officinalis* 'Icterina') with broad leaves beautifully marked with gold and green.

be happy to provide a good flavour and fresh aroma. Coloured-leaved forms and *S. rutilans* make good container plants but dislike too much water.

Propagation: Summer cuttings or layers. Sometimes the old bush will layer naturally or seed for *S. officinalis* itself; cuttings for *S. rutilans*.

Salad burnet
(*Sanguisorba minor*) Rosaceae
A short-lived dainty perennial which forms first a rosette of leaves, then branching pink stems to 30 cm (12 in) with long mid-green leaves growing alternately along it. Flowers appear for midsummer as small globular heads of red and green with red protruding styles.

Part used: Leaves as an addition to salads and summer drinks. Medicinally as a styptic herb.
Cultivation: Most soils are suitable including chalk and limestone. Cut back stems after flowering to encourage stronger rosettes the following spring.
Propagation: Seed or division of rootstock, preferably in spring.

Savory, bean herb
(*Satureia species*) Labiatae
There are two distinct forms of savory. Winter savory (*Satureia montana*) is a small bushy evergreen perennial 30 cm (12 in) high with dark green leaves in opposite pairs and small pink-mauve flowers from midsummer. Summer savory (*S. hortensis*) is an annual, growing up to 30 cm (12 in) high, with larger, light green leaves and more conspicuous pale pink flowers in midsummer.

Part used: Leaves for culinary flavouring and in pot-pourri.
Cultivation: Winter savory needs a well-drained soil whereas summer savory is really more reliable on good garden soil in a warm corner, or even in a container in colder areas. Both like sunshine, good light and hate frost. Trim back winter savory after flowering and treat it to a thin dressing of compost in the autumn.
Propagation: Winter savory from summer cuttings or seed. Summer savory from seed sown with protection in late spring.

Soapwort, bouncing bet, fuller's herb
(*Saponaria officinalis*) Caryophyllaceae
A hardy perennial with stiff stems 45–60 cm (18–24 in) high, and pale green smooth leaves held in

▶ Young shoots of variegated lemon balm (*Melissa officinalis* 'Aurea') in a container enhance a bed of herbs.

pairs along the stem and rising from swollen joints. The flowers are a pale rose pink in late summer, either single or fully double in clustered heads at the top of stems, faintly scented and spicy like garden pinks. This plant has served as a natural detergent for centuries and today is employed in conservation of delicate and antique fabrics and embroidery where vegetable dyes have been included. (Fresh shoots agitated in water provide a soapy froth).

The name 'soapwort' was given by William Turner in the sixteenth century who gave vernacular names to several wild plants where none had been known previously (see page 8).

Part used: Whole shoots as a mild detergent.

Cultivation: It is tolerant of poor soils including chalk and will grow in some shade. It needs to be allowed to spread and make a good patch for effectiveness.

Propagation: Pull away the offshoots in spring or divide the rootstock in autumn or spring.

Sorrel

(*Rumex* species) Polygonaceae

Hardy perennial plants undaunted by poor conditions or adverse weather, up to 90 cm (36 in) high, forming a tap root and with arrow-shaped bright green leaves clasping the reddish tough stem. The flowers are reddish-green-brown in loose terminal spikes throughout the summer.

Buckler's sorrel (*R. scutatus*), is a smaller plant at 45 cm (18 in), with kidney-shaped more delicate green leaves and similar flowers over a long period in summer. Generally regarded as weeds of cultivation, when sorrels are well grown the leaves make a good addition to salads for their thirst-quenching quality and sharp apple-lemon flavour.

Part used: Leaves for culinary flavouring.

Cultivation: Fertile soil with some moisture-

· HANDY HINT ·

There are innumerable species of southernwood (*Artemisia*) with varying aromatic qualities. Why not make a collection? They are among the most ancient of herbs and their silvery green foliage looks wonderful when drenched with raindrops; pure garden enchantment in the moonlight.

---

retentive material. Will tolerate shade. Remove flowers and seed heads to maintain a continuing supply of fresh leaves. Pick the outer leaves to retain the growing point of the plant.

Propagation: Seed in situ, thin seedlings to about 25 cm (10 in) apart or alternatively in trays for transplanting.

Southernwood, lad's love

(*Artemisia abrotanum*) Compositae

A hardy semi-evergreen which forms a small flowerless woody bush 60 cm–1 m (2–3¼ ft) high with soft dark green thread-like foliage, aromatic of sweet camphor. Somewhat knarled in appearance during winter in cold districts.

Part used: The feathery foliage, dried as an insect repellent.

Cultivation: Give it a light well-drained soil containing some moisture-retentive material in full sun. An attractive herb for a large container, for patio or balcony.

Propagation: Take hardwood cuttings in the latter part of the summer; or sow seed, then plant out seedlings at least 90 cm (36 in) apart.

Sweet Cicely, anise fern

(*Myrrhis odorata*) Umbelliferae

An erect perennial up to 1 m (3¼ ft) high with soft fern-like foliage scented of aniseed or licorice.

Flowers are white in late spring and early summer, followed by long upstanding seeds.

Part used: Leaves used to flavour salads or to sweeten cooked fruits (useful for diabetic diets). Seed as a flavouring. Root as a vegetable.

Cultivation: Select a moist soil, slightly acid and deeply worked where there is some shade. Avoid a corner that gets the early morning sun, as sweet Cicely is the earliest herb to break in the spring, and damage is done to frosted plants by the sun if they are not given time to thaw out naturally.

Propagation: Sow seed in autumn. It will self sow readily. Root cuttings may be taken in winter.

Tansy, feverfew and costmary
(*Tanacetum* species) Compositae
Closely related these three plants are very different in the garden.

Tansy (*Tanacetum vulgare*) is an erect, tough, hardy perennial up to 1.2 m (4 ft) high and on close inspection there is considerable variation in foliage patterns among plants from one clone to another. The leaves are a dark bright green, handsome, feather shaped but not feathery. They are deeply divided, pungent and spicy. Flowers are dark yellow, held in flattish heads above the foliage and resemble buttons because there are no petals. An invasive plant.

Feverfew (*T. parthenium*) is a prettier cottage plant which enjoys present-day renown as giving relief from migraine. A compact, bushy, short-lived perennial 45 cm (18 in) high with lime green leaves deeply divided but triangular in general shape. Flowers appear throughout the summer, daisy-like with chalk-white rounded petals. There is a gold-leaved form *T.p. aureum* and double-flowered cultivars 'Plenum' and 'White Bonnet'.

Costmary or alecost (*T. balsamita*) is a hardy perennial that disappears totally below ground in the winter, leaving a woody stem which snuggles beneath the soil surface. In spring growth pushes up to 90 cm (36 in), forming a bushy, somewhat lax plant with pale green leaves, ovate with rounded toothed edges. Flowers are borne in small flat clusters at the top of the stem, yellow and like tansy (*T. vulgare*) devoid of petals. It is commonly confused with the camphor plant (*Balsamita vulgaris*) which has white flowers and greyer leaves).

Part used: Leaves, tansy as an insecticide and feverfew medicinally. Alecost was used for strewing.

Cultivation: Introduce tansy with caution as it makes off for the opposite side of the garden wherever it is planted. Any garden soil is suitable where there is some sunshine. Feverfew prefers the border edge, or pathway or gravel where its roots can get into something cool with its head in the sunshine. A lovely edging plant if kept renewed. Alecost needs a well drained fertile soil and if it is deprived of sunshine does not flower. A very invasive plant, which deteriorates as it travels, so needs to be broken up every third or fourth year and the good pieces replanted.

Propagation: Division of rootstock for tansy and seed for feverfew which will self sow about the garden. Division in spring for alecost.

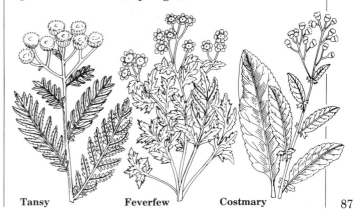

Tansy   Feverfew   Costmary

Tarragon, estragon

(*Artemisia dracunculus*) Compositae

A perennial up to 90 cm (36 in) high where it is happy, with narrow strips of leaves and rarely flowering. Do not confuse it with *A.d.* 'Indora' (also called *A. dracunculoides*), the coarse-growing Russian tarragon.

Part used: Leaves fresh or dried for flavouring.

Cultivation: Select a sunny spot where there is good drainage to prevent lush growth which is inferior in flavour, and does not survive damp chilly winters very well. Protection from frost for the crowns may be needed as it is a true Mediterranean plant.

Propagation: Divide rootstock or take cuttings of young shoots in spring. You will need to renew plants every three years.

Thyme

(*Thymus* species) Labiatae

A low-growing twiggy perennial that hugs the ground 5–20 cm (2–8 in). Leaves are minute, oval, grey-green and highly aromatic.

Thymus caespititius, a hummock-forming plant with pine-scented leaves and tiny purplish flowers in early summer. The entire plant is minute and lends itself to cultivation in a pot.

T. × *citriodorus* a lemon-scented spreading little bush with smooth green leaves and good in its form 'Variegatus' in which the leaves are edged with silver.

T. herba-barona the caraway-scented thyme is mat forming and semi prostrate, straggling over the ground, but is useful for growing in walls or along steps.

T. serpyllum, known as the mother of thyme is, in fact, the English wild thyme and one com-monly encountered for gardens in cultivars such as 'Pink Chintz' with pure pink flowers in early summer; 'Coccinea', red flowers; and 'Albus', white flowers and paler foliage, flowering at the same time as distinct forms.

The common thyme or garden thyme (*T. vulgaris*) is the one to grow for good culinary flavour. It forms cushions of growth like little hummocks up to 30 cm (12 in), as opposed to the carpeting habit of other thymes. The cultivars 'Aureus' with yellow-green leaves and 'Variegata' with grey-green overall appearance, are ones that are commonly grown.

Part used: Leaves as culinary flavouring and in the production of oils such as thymol. Add to pot-pourri with restraint.

Cultivation: All thymes love warm dry soil with a good deal of sun and when given these conditions the aroma is stronger than from plants cultivated in shade and on heavier soils. Clip hard back in the autumn to encourage fresh lively growth the following spring. Ideal plants for using in association with paving or in a front-of-the-border position with good drainage.

Propagation: Summer cuttings (tips) or division of crowns, or layer in late summer.

Valerian, phew plant

(*Valerian officinalis*) Valerianaceae

A pretty perennial up to 1.5 m (5 ft) high with dark green regularly divided leaves and pale pink flowers in clusters at the top of a solitary stem in midsummer. The conical root has fibrous offshoots when mature at the end of summer and is lifted in autumn when required.

Part used: Root occasionally used for medicinal purposes.

Cultivation: Tolerant of most soils, where there is some sun during the day.

Propagation: Division of the rootstock.

◀ **Informality is established by irregular paving and gravel and varied plant form in the herb garden.**

Vervain, herb of grace

(*Verbena officinalis*) Verbenaceae
An odourless perennial (which is unusual in the herb collection). Up to 90 cm (36 in) with a particularly upright stance, dark toothed leaves, prominently veined and paler below. The flower stem branches to hold spikes of small clustered pale mauve flowers in summer, over a long period. Its uses are vague but it has retained prominence for its magical properties and association with religious ceremonies as an altar plant. It is supposed to have grown on the hill of Calvary.
Part used: Leaves and flower heads as a cleansing wash.
Cultivation: It likes a fairly dry soil in some sun.
Propagation: Division of the fibrous rootstock.

Violet, sweet violet, heartsease

(*Viola* species) Violaceae
Heartsease, wild pansy (*V. tricolor*), is a short-lived creeping perennial 15 cm (6 in) high with small dark green triangular leaves and tiny pansy-like flowers held well above all summer with purple, cream and yellow in various colour combinations. It has an ancient reputation for being a substitute for litmus in acid/alkaline tests. It is a good edging plant when grown in colonies.
Part used: Flowers crystallized or made into syrup. Small hardy perennials up to 15 cm (6 in), all violas are dainty plants. Sweet violet (*V. odorata*) has shiny deep green, heart-shaped leaves that emit the scent before the flowers bloom. The spurred flowers are borne singly, held well above the foliage from early spring, with five petals, the lower one rounded. There is a white-flowered form *V.o.* 'Alba' and a wide range of viola species and cultivars, although *V.odorata* is the true herb and the only sweet-scented one.
Cultivation: All violas like a moist humus-rich soil and a semi-shaded spot.
Propagation: Seed when available. Division of roots and pieces of plant with tiny roots can be detached and planted out.

Wall germander and wood sage

(*Teucrium* species) Labiatae
Wall germander (*Teucrium chamaedrys*) is a sweet-smelling perennial up to 25 cm (10 in), with dark green, deeply veined and toothed leaves with a thick, shiny appearance. Flowers are pink-purple in summer. The great asset of this plant is that it can be clipped to form a tiny hedge and thus it makes a good formal edge to beds in the garden. It was popular in knot gardens in the sixteenth century.

Wood sage (*T. scorodonia*) is a perennial herb with a creeping rootstock and stems up to 45 cm (18 in), with dull green sage-like leaves, wrinkled and oval, and paler below. Pale greenish-buff flowers have long purple anthers and are carried to one side of the leafless stalk. It smells of hops.
Part used: Leaves to make a blood-cleansing infusion.
Cultivation: Wall germander will grow in any good fertile soil provided it is well drained.

Violet

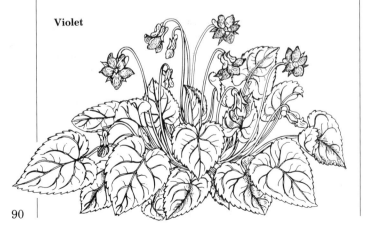

Sometimes it is difficult to get going. Wood sage, on the other hand, prefers semi-shade.
Propagation: Summer cuttings for wall germander and division of rootstock for wood sage in spring.

Wormwood
(*Artemisia absinthium*) Compositae
A hardy perennial with pale silver, deeply divided foliage reaching about 90 cm (36 in) but can be restricted. Leaves are richly aromatic and camphorous, downy beneath. Tiny clusters of dull yellow flowers appear in summer. Good gleaming white foliage in the cultivar 'Lambrook Silver'.
Part used: Dried foliage for its worm-expelling properties, or as an insecticide in cupboards.
Cultivation: Tolerant of all but the heaviest soils, it prefers some sunshine but will not come amiss in a north-facing border and seems not to mind a draughty position. Grow several plants together for good effect. Cut back in the early spring to retain fresh growth of a better colour.
Propagation: Divide the rootstock or sow seed, or take softwood cuttings in summer from established plants.

Yarrow, sneezewort
(*Achillea millefolium*) Compositae
A tough hardy perennial up to 60 cm (24 in) high with narrow, dark green, much-divided leaves that are aromatic. Flowers are white with varying degrees of pink tinge, appearing from early spring throughout the year. Tends to sprawl and look untidy.
Part used: Leaves and stems to staunch bleeding or to include in snuff to clear the head.
Cultivation: Choose a sunny spot on any garden soil; tolerant of stony ground.
Propagation: Divide the creeping rootstock or sow seed.

POISONOUS HERBS
Some herbs are extremely powerful in their action upon the human body, and while they are recognized in orthodox and homeopathic medicine, extreme care should be exercised in growing them. Everyone needs to be able to recognize dangerous plants and great care needs to be taken in handling them. It is not too fussy to suggest that gloves be worn when handling some plants such as aconite (*Aconitum napellus*), especially if there is an abrasion of the skin. Drastic reactions are not unknown and it should not be forgotten that some herbal anaesthetics and hallucinatory inducers have been the foundation for magic and witchcraft in the past, and caused death.

Black hellebore, Christmas rose
(*Helleborus niger*) Ranunculaceae
The whole plant is poisonous; an extract from the root is used in homeopathic medicine. A hardy perennial 60 cm (24 in) tall, with large leathery leaves that form a clump above delicate white flowers, sometimes spotted purple or pink within and carried on robust stems in mid-winter. A useful herb for the garden proper where it likes to be left undisturbed.

Deadly nightshade, belladonna
(*Artropa belladonna*) Solanaceae
All parts of the plant are poisonous. The sweet juicy berries are attractive to children. A shrubby straggling perennial up to 2 m (6¾ ft) with oval leaves and purple bell-shaped fluted flowers, with a paler shade on the outside. Somewhat sinister. Used to be used by courtesans to enlarge the pupils of the eyes and make them more attractive.

Foxglove (see page 71)
(*Digitalis purpurea*) Scrophulariaceae
Even today there is no synthetic drug to replace

91

Foxgloves (*Digitalis purpurea*), growing with opium poppies (*Papaver somniferum*) and melilot (*Melilotis officinalis*).

the value of the foxglove in cardiac therapy. The active principle is contained in the leaves, which are soft and hairy beneath, and not to be confused with those of comfrey (*Symphytum officinalis*) which are bristly beneath and not poisonous.

Henbane

(*Hysocamus niger*) Solanaceae
The plant is highly poisonous in every part. A biennial that produces a rosette of leaves the first season, then a very hairy stem up to 90 cm (36 in) the following year. The leaves are grey green, coarsely toothed, hairy and sticky to touch. Funnel-shaped flowers appear on one side of the stem in summer and are likely to evoke suspicion with their dirty yellow colour marked with purple veins and spots. The plant has an unpleasant odour and has long been linked with witchcraft because of its hallucinatory properties.

Leopard's bane, mountain tobacco

(*Arnica montana*) Compositae
Both flowers and root supply the drug arnica. A biennial, a rosette of ribbed leaves forms the first year, followed by attractive bright yellow daisies the next, up to 60 cm (24 in) high. The whole plant is aromatic.

Lily-of-the-valley

(*Convallaria majalis*) Liliaceae.
All parts of the plant are poisonous; the active constituents are obtained from the late summer red berries. A hardy perennial, spreading quickly by creeping underground stems. Twin broad green leaves up to 15–25 cm (6–10 in) long appear in spring followed by a leafless stem bearing one-sided spike of dainty white hanging bells, deliciously scented in late spring.

Monkshood, aconite (see page 67)

(*Aconitum napellus*) Ranunculaceae
All parts are poisonous, especially the root.

Thornapple, jimson weed

(*Datura stramonium*) Solanaceae
Seeds and leaves are particularly poisonous. A bushy annual that is of very sinister appearance. Large dark green jagged leaves that curve hide a thick stem up to 30–45 cm (12–18 in) high and an upstanding white folded funnel-shaped flower up to 10 cm (4 in) in length which opens at night and is fragrant. Followed by a spiny capsule rather like a horse chestnut, which when ripe expels brown-black seeds.

· CULINARY HERBS AND THEIR USES ·

Name	Part	Use
Angelica (*Angelica archangelica*)	Stem	Crystallized, seed desserts and syrups
Basil (*Ocimum basilicum*)	Leaves	Soups, stuffings, pasta, fish, teas, liqueurs
Bay (*Laurus nobilis*)	Leaves	Stews, stuffings, meat, poultry, chutneys
Caraway (*Carum carvi*)	Seed	Sauces, vegetables, savoury rice, confectionery, bread
Chervil (*Anthriscus cerefolium*)	Leaves	Soups, salads, eggs, poultry, garnish
Chives (*Allium schoenoprasm*)	Leaves	Salads, eggs, cheese, soup garnish
Coriander (*Coriandrum sativum*)	Leaves	Salads, sandwiches, dairy produce, meat, curries, drinks
	Seed	Soups, vegetables, pasta, baking
Dill (*Anethum graveolens*)	Leaves	Vegetables, dairy produce, garnish
	Seed	Stews, chowders, sauces, fish, vinegars
Fennel (*Foeniculum vulgare*)	Leaves	Soups, fish, eggs, meat, pickles
	Seed	Soups, cheese, fish, poultry
Garlic (*Allium sativum*)	Bulb	Soups, stews, stuffings, meat, game, pickles, butter
Lemon balm (*Melissa officinalis*)	Leaves	Stuffings, drinks

Name	Part	Use
Lovage (*Levisticum originale*)	Leaves	Rice dishes, eggs, fish, meat, vinegars
	Stems	Stews, stuffings
Marjoram (*Origanum* species)	Leaves	Chowders, stuffings, salads, meat poultry, drinks, chutney
Mint, various (*Mentha* species)	Leaves	Soups, sauces, dressings, meat, poultry, drinks, garnish, desserts
Parsley (*Petroselinum crispum*)	Leaves	Soups, sauces, salads, sandwiches, garnish
Rosemary (*Rosmarinus officinalis*)	Leaves	Stews, pasta, eggs, meat, vinegars, liqueurs, garnish
Sage (*Salvia officinalis*)	Leaves	Stews, stuffings, meat, poultry, game, teas
Savory: winter (*Satureja montana*); summer (*Satureja hortensis*)	Leaves	Salads, sandwiches, pasta, eggs, fish, desserts, teas
Sorrel (*Rumex acetosa*)	Leaves	Salads, sandwiches
Sweet Cicely (*Myrrhis odorata*)	Seed	Desserts, jellies, jams
Tarragon (*Artemisia dracunculus*)	Leaves	Soups, stews, stuffings, eggs, meat, poultry, vinegars
Thyme (*Thymus vulgaris*)	Leaves	Soups, stews, stuffings, fish, meat, teas, liqueurs

· HERBS AND THEIR USES ·

For medicinal use

Name	Flowers
Agrimony (*Agrimonia eupatoria*)	Small yellow
Angelica (*Angelica archangelica*)	Tiny yellowish
Arnica (*Arnica montana*)*	Daisy, yellow
Betony (*Stachys officinalis*)	Rose pink
Burdock (*Arctium lappa*)	Purple red bobbles
Chamomile (*Chamaemelum nobile*)	Daisy, white
Comfrey (*Symphytum officinale*)	Blue/pink
Deadly nightshade (*Atropa belladonna*)*	Purplish brown
Dill (*Anethum graveolens*)	Tiny yellow
Elderberry (*Sambucus nigra*)	Cream, dainty
Elecampane (*Inula helenium*)	Bright yellow
Evening primrose (*Oenothera biennis*)	Yellow
Feverfew (*Tanacetum parthenium*)	Daisy, white
Foxglove (*Digitalis purpurea*)*	Purple pink
Gentian (*Gentiana lutea*)	Yellow
Hellebore (*Helleborus niger*)*	White
Henbane (*Hyoscyamus niger*)*	Yellow, purple-veined
Horehound (*Marrubium vulgare*)	Dusty white
Houseleek (*Sempervivum tectorum*)	White
Hyssop (*Hyssopus officinalis*)	Blue
Lavender (*Lavandula angustifolia*)	Mauve
Licorice (*Glycyrrhiza glabra*)	Lilac
Lily-of-the-valley (*Convallaria majalis*)*	White
Lungwort (*Pulmonaria officinalis*)	Blue/pink
Meadowsweet (*Filipendula ulmaria*)	Cream
Melilot (*Melilotus officinalis*)	Yellow
Monkshood (*Aconitum napellus*)*	Blue
Motherwort (*Leonorus cardiaca*)	Mauve
Nettle (*Urtica dioica*)	Green
Opium poppy (*Papaver somniferum*)*	Pink
Orpine (*Hylotelephium telephium*)	Deep pink
Peppermint (*Mentha × piperita*)	Mauve
Pokeroot (*Phytolacca americanum*)	White/pink
Rhubarb (*Rheum officinale*)	Cream
Rose (*Rosa canina*)	Pink
Sage (*Salvia officinalis*)	Mauve pink
St Johns wort (*Hypericum perforatum*)	Yellow
Selfheal (*Prunella vulgaris*)	Pink
Violet (*Viola odorata*)	Mauve
Yarrow (*Achillea millefolium*)	Daisy, white

*Poisonous

For dyes

Name	Dye colour
Agrimony (*Agrimonia eupatoria*)	Tawny to brown-grey
Alkanet (*Alkanna tinctoria*)	Red
Anthemis (*Anthemis tinctoria*)	Orange to red-brown
Bloodroot (*Sanguisorba canadensis*)	Red
Broom (*Genista tinctoria*)	Yellow
Elder (*Sambucus nigra*)	Dusky blue
Broom (*Cytisus scoparius*)	Yellow
Lily-of-the-valley (*Convallaria majalis*)	Green, yellow-gold
Madder (*Rubia tinctoria*)	Coral to deep red-brown
Meadowsweet (*Filipendula ulmaria*)	Greenish yellow
Nettle (*Urtica dioica*)	Yellow
Pokeroot (*Phytolacca americana*)	Purple
Sorrel (*Rumex acetosa*)	Dark yellow
Weld (*Reseda luteola*)	Yellow
Woad (*Isatis tinctoria*)	Blue

For pot-pourri

Name	Flower colour
Bergamot (*Monarda didyma*)**	Red
Catnip (*Nepeta cataria*)**	White
Chamomile (*Chamaemelum nobile*)**	White
Costmary (*Tanacetum balsamita*)**	Yellow cream
Cowslip (*Primula veris*)	Yellow
Evening primrose (*Oenothera biennis*)	Yellow
Hyssop (*Hyssopus officinalis*)**	Blue
Jasmine (*Jasminum officinalis*)	White
Lavender (*Lavandula angustifolia*)**	Mauve
Lily-of-the-valley (*Convallaria majalis*)	White
Lemon balm (*Melissa officinalis*)**	White
Marjoram (*Onites* species)**	Pink
Melilot (*Melilotus officinalis*)	Yellow
Mint (*Mentha* species)**	Mauve
Myrtle (*Myrtus communis*)	White
Pelargonium (*Pelargonium* species)**	Pinks
Pink (*Dianthus caryophyllus*)	Pinks
Rose (*Rosa gallica*)	Pink/red
Rosemary (*Rosmarinus officinalis*)**	Blue
Soapwort (*Saponaria officinalis*)	Pale pink
Southernwood (*Artemisia abrotanum*)**	Does not flower
Thyme (*Thymus* species)	Mauve
Wall germander (*Teucrium chamaedrys*)**	Blue
Woodruff (*Asperula odorata*)**	White
Wormwood (*Artemisia absinthium*)**	Green

**Use leaves also

Index

Page numbers in *italics* indicate an illustration or boxed table.
See also A–Z of Herbs, 65–92.